THE IMPORTANCE OF UNCONDITIONAL TRUST IN GOD

All inquiries should be addressed to:

Book Domain LLC.
543 E Louise Dr Phoenix, Az 85050

Ordering Information:
Amount Deals. Special rebates are accessible on the amount bought by corporations, associations, and others. For points of interest, contact the distributor at the address above.

Printed in the United States of America.

ISBN-13   Paperback   978-1-96410-095-1
           eBook   978-1-96410-094-4

Library of Congress Control Number: 2025902916

THE IMPORTANCE OF UNCONDITIONAL TRUST IN GOD

EDWARD LAPOINTE

BOOK DOMAIN LLC
Publish to Perfection

INTRODUCTION

My intent for this writing is to help you get a better understanding of why it is Important to Trust God unconditionally.

First you need to understand who you are getting this information from. I am not a well-established author nor do I have a PhD. I am not a Pastor, I am not a Prophet, and I am not an Evangelists. I would like to believe I have a little knowledge and experience in living this Christian life for a period of about 25 years.

I have read numbers and numbers of books on Christian topics; I have studied the Word and will be using and giving you Scriptures verifying and basing what I write on Scriptural truth. My hope is you will, not only, read through the Scriptures, but that you'll pause and meditate on them and even research them. The more knowledge, wisdom and insight you have can only benefit you.

Remember; do not base, or make a decision upon what to read and one Scripture. It is said; let a matter be established by two or three witnesses. When you find a Scripture that stands out to you look elsewhere in the Word for verification of that Scripture. Scripture always confirms Scripture with Scripture.

When I am writing on a topic in this book I will write at least two Scriptures to verify and establish what I'm writing about.

I will write some of my personal experiences in life. And if you decide to, you can purchase and read my memoir: His Grace in the Midst of Tragedy. To read that one and/or this one will be your decision. I will do my best to present the truth.

This writing is primarily for the new Christian. My hope is; that it will help jump start you into a little more spiritual progress, a little faster then it took me, but not too fast. I guess it's really just a matter of how bad do you want it.

It won't work if you have one foot in the world and the other in Christ. We are in this world, but we are not of it. We are of a heavenly kingdom.

Jesus prayed in John 17: 14-15 (NLT)

> *I have given them your word. And the world hates them because they do not belong to the world, just as I do not belong to the world. I am not asking you to take them out of the world; but to keep them safe from the evil one.*

> Matthew 10:25 (NLT). *Students are to be like their teacher, and slaves are to be like their master. And since I the master of the household, have been called the prince of demons, the members of my household will be called by even worse names!* (My emphasis).

Are you ready for your journey? Here we go.

CHAPTER 1

THE BEGINNING

Are you willing to be **ALL** in? because, it takes faith to trust Him unconditionally. It takes faith and trust to surrender your will and following and obeying God's will.

As a former Marine I did not like the word surrender. It was instilled into us to never surrender to the enemy. Backup, and re-group if necessary; but never surrender.

The same is necessary in the spiritual; never surrender to the devil and his cohorts. First of all, he's a defeated foe; Jesus made sure of that.

But, and its a big BUT; we are to surrender our will and replace it with God's will.

Remember; Our goal is to become like Jesus. This goal can only become achievable by doing and obeying His Word.

The Apostle James said in James 1:22 (NLT)

But don't just listen to God's word. You must do what it says. Otherwise, you are only fooling yourselves.

Matthew 7:24 *Anyone who listens to my teaching and follows it is wise, like a person who builds a house on solid rock.* (My emphasis).

I have been fooling myself in a lot of areas where I am a listener and not a doer!

Much of this is caused because I haven't been doing what the Apostle Paul said to do in Romans 12:2 (NLT)

Don't copy the behavior and costumes of this world, but let God transform you into a new person by changing the way you think. Then you will learn to know God's will for you, which is good and pleasing and perfect (My emphasis).

Paul wrote in 2 Corinthians 6:14-18 (NLT)

Don't team up with those who are unbelievers. How can righteousness be a partner with wickedness? How can light live with darkness?

What harmony can there be between Christ and the devil? How can a believer be a partner with an unbeliever?

And what agreement has the temple of God with idols? For you are the temple of the living God. As God has said: "I will dwell in them and walk among them. I will be their God, and they shall be my people."

Therefore, come out from among unbelievers, and separate yourselves from them, says the Lord. Don't touch their filthy things, and I will welcome you.

And I will be your father, and you will be my sons and daughters, says the Lord Almighty (My emphasis).

Growing up I remember these sayings: trust has to be earned. And: it sounds too good to be true or: I'll believe it when I see it. Have you heard these at some point in your life? They may be true with people, but are not true with God. If He says such and such is going to happen; it will happen.

If He promises you something and you meet the conditions, concerning that promise, no matter how impossible it looks or sounds, it will come to pass.

But also, what I have learned is, the more faith you have, the more you'll trust Him, and, the more you trust Him, the more you'll obey Him. And when the promise comes to fruition; it increases your faith to start believing for bigger and better promises. You can trust Him.

Proverbs 3:5-7 (NLT). *Trust in the Lord with all your heart; do not depend on your own understanding.*

Seek his will in all you do, and he will show you which path to take.

Don't be impressed with your own wisdom. Instead, fear the Lord and turn away from evil.

Then you will have healing for your body and strength for your bones.

You don't have to be All in to be saved. Ephesians 2:8-9 (NLT)

God saved you by his grace when you believed. And you can't take credit for this; it is a gift from God.

Salvation is not a reward for the good things we have done, so none of us can boast about it.

Romans 3:24 (NLT) *Yes God, with undeserved kindness, declares that we are righteous. He did this through Christ Jesus when he freed us from the penalty of our sins* (My emphasis).

God's Word is full of stories about people just like you and me, who, when they trusted and obeyed God, and did what He asked them to do, no matter how crazy it seemed, they came out of it blessed. And God's will was accomplished.

God said in, Isaiah 55:11 (NLT)

It is the same with My word. I send it out, and it always produces fruit. It will accomplish all I wanted it to, and it will prosper everywhere I send it.

Deuteronomy 32:2 (NLT). Let *my teaching fall on you like rain; let my speech settle like dew. Let my words fall like rain on tender grass, my gentle showers on young plants.* (My emphasis).

The more your obedient to do what He asks, the more He blesses you. Don't look at it as something you've earned; because you can't earn it. It's just who God is; you can't out give God.

Also, being all in does not mean perfection; it means progress. Your entire journey will be a faith and trust journey. A lot of three steps forward, two steps back, a continuous learning adventure.

Our goal is to grow into the full stature of Jesus Christ; I don't believe we will come to that full stature until we go home to be with Him, or until He comes back for His church. But, I want to come as close to being like Him as I possibly can, while I am still here.

Trust appears many times throughout the Bible. Here are just a couple of Scriptures;

> Isaiah 26:3 (NLT) *You will keep in perfect peace all who trust in you, all whose thoughts are fixed on you!*

> Psalms 37:3-6 (NLT) *Trust in the Lord and do good. Then you will live safely in the land and prosper.*
> *Take delight in the Lord, and he will give you your hearts desires.*
> *He will make your innocence radiate like the dawn, and the justice of your cause will shine like the noonday sun* (My emphasis).

Why should we trust God unconditionally? The answer is obvious; because of what He has done for us. Christ came in the likeness of human flesh. He was all God and all human.

For 33 years He walked the earth declaring and showing with signs and wonders that the Jews, at the time Christ walked the earth had never seen. They had only heard or read about these kinds of miracles through the books of the Old Testament.

Many believed on Him, but many did not, mostly religious folks. They thought he did these signs by the power of the devil. (It's amazing how the devil can get credit for someone doing good things).

The Bible is very clear; John 10:10 (NLT)

> *The thief's purpose is to steal and kill and destroy. My purpose is to give them a rich and satisfying life.*

The Scripture just above that, 10:9 says;

> *yes, I am the gate. Those who come in through me will be saved. They will come and go freely and will find good pasture.*

Even when He was crucified, Jesus prayed to the Father; Luke 23:34 (NLT)

> *Jesus said, "Father, forgive them, for they don't know what they are doing." And the soldiers gambled for his clothes by throwing dice.* Those must have been expensive clothes (My emphasis).

This is the primary reason I trust Him unconditionally. If He did all this for me and you, how can we not trust Him. He wants the very best for us.

This is a little off the subject, but I feel I need to write it down. I had wondered. how Jesus went through His life and never committed sin? Then I read in the Romans 5:12-19 (NLT)

> *When Adam sinned, sin entered the world. Adam's sin brought death, so death spread to everyone, for everyone sinned.*
>
> *Yes, people sinned even before the law was given. But it was not counted as sin because there was not yet any law to break.*

Still, everyone died from the time of Adam to the time of Moses, even those who did not disobey an explicit commandment of God, as Adam did. Now, Adam is a symbol; a representation of Christ who was yet to come.

But there is a great difference between Adam's sin and God's gracious gift. For the sin of this one man, Adam, brought death to many. But even greater is God's wonderful grace in his gift of forgiveness to many through this one man, Jesus Christ.

And the result of God's gracious gift is very different from the result of that one man's sin. For Adam's sin led to condemnation, but God's free gift leads to our being made right with God, even though we are guilty of many sins.

For the sin of this one man, Adam, caused death to rule over many. But even greater is God's wonderful grace and his gift of righteousness, for all who receive it will live in triumph over sin and death through this one man, Jesus Christ.

Yes, Adam's one sin brings condemnation for everyone, but Christ's one act of righteousness brings a right relationship with God and a new life for everyone.

Because one person disobeyed God, many became sinners. But because one other person obeyed God, many were made righteous (My emphasis).

So, this said to me that through Adam every person carries the sin nature. Then how come Jesus never sinned, He was tempted on every point just as we are, yet without sin.

Then I realized that we are all the seed of Adam. Accept one; that is the man Jesus. He was the seed of God; He did not have the sin nature!

We all have our own testimonies of how we were born again; each and every one of the Christians in the world have their own unique testimony.

My advice to new Christians is not to go too fast; I tell you this from my own experience of going too fast.

I'm not sure how many born-again believers started out as I did? My unique testimony is that since 1976 I have had a mental disorder. When I was born again in 1998 I received the healing of my chronic bronchitis. Where I made my mistake was that I also believed I had received the healing of my mental illness.

This was a mistake that cost me dearly; four years in the psychiatric hospital for stopping my medication. This did not happen quickly, first, I talked my psychiatrist into lowering my medication. Then the descent was slow and steady. Soon I had what they call religious ideations. I began to think I was a Prophet, I thought I knew everything; when in reality I knew hardly anything.

When I arrived at the hospital I began to blame everyone, my psychiatrist, my psychologist, my pastor and the Prophet; this is called: *taking offense.*

The original meaning of offense is to bait. When trappers use to bait their traps it was called: to take offense.

This is one of the primary weapons of deceit the enemy uses. It's a lie; he is a liar. And that's all he knows how to do. If we take the bait it will open a whole new can of worms. If he can get you to take the bait of offense he will hit you with other character defects, such as; strife, bitterness, anger, hatred and so on. My advice is; don't take the bait!

The truth is, I had no one to blame but myself. And the truth is; God had to cool my heels, because I was way out of line, and could've hurt the body of Christ. Trying to teach people something I didn't know myself, doing that could have stopped people from getting saved by learning I was only telling half-truths. Yes, God needed to slow me down.

Here's the good news; during those four years God redirected my life for the better and has been doing it ever since. That hospital stay was my first experience in learning to trust God unconditionally and I don't regret that four-year stay at all.

The two paragraphs above were my first experience of the chastening (correction) of the Lord. This was a severe correction; which was what I needed. I have received correction many times, but the more I grow in the Lord the corrections have become less and less.

If you are in the center of God's will you will not need to be corrected; because you will be doing His will. Here is a Scripture for it;

> Hebrews 12:6-8,11 (NLT) *For the Lord disciplines those He loves, and He punishes each one He accepts as His child.*
>
> *As you endure this divine discipline, remember that the Lord is treating you as His own children.*
>
> *Whoever heard of a child who is never disciplined by his father? If God doesn't discipline you as He does all of His children, it means that you are illegitimate and are not really His children at all.*
>
> *No discipline is enjoyable when it is happening, it's painful! But afterward there will be a peaceful harvest of right living for those who are trained in this way* (My emphasis).

God's word says in 1 Peter 5:10 (NLT)

> *In His kindness God called you to share in His eternal glory by means of Christ Jesus. So after you have suffered*

a little while, He will restore, support, and strengthen you, and He will place you on a firm foundation (My emphasis).

Paul wrote in Romans 12:3 (NLT), describing exactly what I did; here is what the Scripture says;

Because of the privilege and authority God has given me, I give each of you this warning: don't think you are better than you really are. Be honest in your evaluation of yourselves, measuring yourselves by the faith God has given us.

I realize that not all Christians have a mental disorder, hopefully very few.

This still does not negate the cost of going too fast. My suggestion is to take it slow, read your Bible, read books on Christian topics, attend church and try to get a Christian mentor in your life.

I did not have these, I thought I could do it alone. A Christian alone is a prime target for the enemy, especially one with very little Bible knowledge truth and power.

Always remember this; you are now a child of God and He is for you, not against you. No matter how bad it gets. Trust Him.

He may not take you out of the water but He will not let you drown, if you go through the fire He will be with you. He will never leave you nor forsake you; TRUST HIM!

Psalms 34:19 *Many are the afflictions of the righteous, but the Lord delivers them out of them all* (My emphasis).

One thing I have learned; ALL in the Bible means all.

2 Corinthians 4:17 (NLT) *For our present troubles are small and won't last very long. Yet they produce for us a glory that vastly outweighs them and will last forever!*

In John 16:33 (NLT) Jesus said, *"I have told you all this so that you may have peace in Me. Here on earth you will have many trials and sorrows. But take heart, because I have overcome the world"* (My emphasis).

In James 1:2-4 (NLT) *Dear brothers and sisters, when troubles come your way, consider it an opportunity for great joy.*

For you know that when your faith is tested, your endurance has a chance to grow.

So let it grow, for when your endurance is fully developed, you will be perfect and complete, needing nothing (My emphasis).

1 Peter1:6, 7 (NLT) confirms what James wrote above.

1 Peter says; *So be truly glad. There is wonderful joy ahead, even though you have to endure many trials for a little while. These trials will show that your faith is genuine. It is being tested as fire tests and purifies gold -though your faith is far more precious than mere gold. So when your faith remains strong through many trials, it will bring you much praise and glory and honor on the day when Jesus Christ is revealed to the whole world* (My emphasis).

I have been through many afflictions, much trouble, and far too many temptations to even want to talk about. I have still not reached that place that James speaks of where I am perfect and entire, wanting nothing. I think I'm getting close, but I am not there yet.

I've had to make up my mind that I am not going to give in to the dictates of my flesh and mind; every day I try to do this and I lose the battle every day. The following scripture told me why.

> Romans 7:14-25 (NLT) *So the trouble is not the law, for it is spiritual and good. The trouble is with me, for I am all too human, a slave to sin.*
>
> *I don't really understand myself, for I want to do what is right, but I don't do it. Instead, I do what I hate. But if I know that what I am doing is wrong, this shows that I agree that the law is good.*
>
> *So I am not the one doing wrong; it is sin living in me that does it. And I know that nothing good lives in me, that is, in my sinful nature. I want to do what is right, but I can't.*
>
> *I want to do what is good, but I don't. I don't want to do what is wrong, but I do it, anyway.*
>
> *But if I do what I don't want to do, I am not really the one doing wrong; it is sin living in me that does it.*
>
> *I have discovered this principle of life that when I want to do what is right, I inevitably do what is wrong.*
>
> *I love God's law with all my heart.*
>
> *But there is another power within me that is at war with my mind. This power makes me a slave to the sin that is still within me.*
>
> *Oh, what a miserable person I am! Who will free me from this life that is dominated by sin and death?*
>
> *Thank God! The answer is in Jesus Christ our Lord.*

So you see how it is: in my mind I really want to obey God's law, but because of my sinful nature I am a slave to sin (My emphasis).

It is one thing for others to condemn you, but it is quite different to condemn yourself. Sometimes the condemnation from others causes us to condemn ourselves.

When this happens you will open the door to very negative thoughts and behaviors of yourself; like guilt, unworthiness and unforgiveness of yourself.

This opens yet another door to failure. Every time you start to succeed, the memories of past failures; like failing at a job or a business venture. a lost marriage etc.

This can cause failure in those areas.

Almost all of you know what I'm writing about. You have to understand a very important fact: failure is an event in your life, it's not who you are.

The apostle Paul offers the antidote for self-condemnation in the book of Romans.

Romans 8:1-7 (NLT) *So now there is no condemnation for those who belong to Christ Jesus. And because you belong to Him, the power of the life giving spirit has freed you from the power of sin that leads to death.*

The law of Moses was unable to save us because of the weakness of our sinful nature. So God did what the law could not do. He sent his own Son in a body like the bodies we sinners have. And in that body God declared an end to sin's control over us by giving his Son as a sacrifice for our sins.

He did this so that the just requirement of the law would be fully satisfied for us, who no longer follow our sinful nature but instead follow the Spirit.

So letting your sinful nature control your mind leads to death. But letting the Spirit control your mind leads to life and peace. For the sinful nature is always hostile to God. It never did obey God's laws, and it never will (My emphasis).

Paul said in 1 Corinthians 9:27 (NLT) *I discipline my body like an athlete, training it to do what it should. Otherwise, I fear that after preaching to others I myself might be disqualified* (My emphasis).

When I was 19 years old I went into the United States Marine Corps. In boot camp I went through some of the most physical and mental retraining that few people ever go through and many of them that tried did not make it.

I did make it and at 73 years of age I am still experiencing some of the benefits of that training. Again, Paul wrote in Romans 12 speaking of something like this training.

Romans 12:1,2 (NLT) *And so, dear brothers and sisters, I plead with you to give your bodies to God because of all He has done for you. Let them be a living and holy sacrifice the kind He will find acceptable. This is truly the way to worship Him.*

Don't copy the behavior and costumes of this world, but let God transform you into a new person by changing the way you think. Then you will learn to know God's will for you, which is good and pleasing and perfect (My emphasis).

CHAPTER 2

KNOW WHO YOU ARE AND WHOSE YOU ARE

I'll tell you who you are and whose you are: a child of the most high God.

When you received Christ as your Lord and Savior you were translated from the power of darkness into the kingdom of God's dear Son. (My translation of Colossians 1:13).

Remember in the introduction I wrote that you have to be All In to receive everything God has for you. You don't have to be All In to be saved.

The Bible is clear; in the book of Acts 16:30,31 (NLT) (talking about the centenarian guard)

Then he brought them out and asked, "Sirs, what most I do to be saved?"

They replied, "Believe in the Lord Jesus and you will be saved, along with everyone in your household."

Romans 10:13 (NLT) *For whosoever shall call upon the name of the Lord shall be saved* (My emphasis).

Romans 5:2 (NLT). *Because of our faith, Christ has brought us into this place of undeserved privilege where we now stand, and we confidently and joyfully look forward to sharing God's glory* (My emphasis).

"I read a commentary by David Guzik on Romans 5:2. I want to focus in on the word "**Grace;** (God's undeserved favor towards us) is not only the way salvation comes to us, it is also a description of our present standing before God."

It is not only the beginning principle of the Christian life, it is also the continuing principle of the Christian life. "*We stand* in Romans 52 above, translates a perfect tense, used in this sense of the present, and with the thought of a continuing attitude."

Many Christians begin in grace, but then think they must go on to perfection and maturity by dealing with God on the principle of law, on the ideas of earning and deserving.

A standing in grace reassures us: God's present attitude towards the believer in Christ Jesus is one of favor, seeing them in terms of joy, beauty, and pleasure. He doesn't just love us; He likes us because we are in Jesus.

You should also know, there are eternal rewards.

2 Corinthians 5:10 (NLT) *For we must all stand before Christ to be judged. We will each receive whatever we deserve for the good or evil we have done in this earthly body.*

1 Corinthians 3:13-15 (NLT) *But on the judgment day, fire will reveal what kind of work each builder has done. The fire will show if a person's work has any value.*

If the work survives, the builder will receive a reward. But if the work is burned up, the builder will suffer a great loss. The builder will be saved, but like someone barely escaping through a wall of flames (My emphasis).

That's the reason why I want to be All in!
In 1 Samuel 13:14 (NLT)

"But now your kingdom must end, (speaking of King Saul) for the Lord has sought out a man after His own heart. The Lord has already appointed him to be the leader of his people, because you have not kept the Lord's command"

In case you're wondering; is obedience important to God? In the Old Testament in the book of 1 Samuel 15:22 (NLT)

But Samuel replied, "what is more pleasing to the Lord: your burnt offerings and sacrifices or your obedience to His voice? Listen! Obedience is better than sacrifice, and submission is better than offering the fat of rams (My emphasis).

In Acts 13:22 (NLT)

But God removed Saul and replaced him with David, a man about whom God said, "I have found David son of

Jesse, a man after My own heart. He will do everything I want him to do" (My emphasis).

If you'll notice the last two verses, God had appointed David before David even knew about it.

He called him a man after His own heart. So David was appointed long before he became king, about 13 years before he became king.

How I would love to hear God say: "I was a man after His own heart!"

I would also love to hear Him say to me, on the day that I go home; "well done good and faithful servant!"

I want to strive for that. How about you?

So then, just who are we to God? Romans 8:16-18 (NLT)

For His spirit joins with our spirit to affirm that we are God's children.

And since we are His children, we are His heirs. In fact, together with Christ we are heirs of God's glory.

But if we are to share His glory, we must also share His suffering.

Yet what we suffer now is nothing compared to the glory He will reveal to us later (My emphasis).

What can we expect now that we know we are God's children? I am going to write out 14 scriptures from the book of Deuteronomy in the Old Testament.

Deuteronomy 28:1-14 (NLT) *"If you fully obey the Lord your God and carefully keep all His commands that I am giving you today, the Lord your God will set you high above all the nations (people) of the world."*

You will experience all these blessings if you obey the Lord your God.

Your towns and your fields will be blessed.

Your children and your crops will be blessed the off-spring of your herds and flocks will be blessed.

Your fruit baskets and bread boards will be blessed.

Wherever you go and whatever you do, you will be blessed.

The Lord will conquer your enemies when they attack you. They will attack you from one direction, but they will scatter from you in seven!

The Lord will guarantee a blessing on everything you do and will fill your storehouses with grain. The Lord your God will bless you in the land He is giving you.

If you obey the commands of the Lord your God and will walk in His ways, the Lord will establish you as His holy people as He swore He would do.

Then all the nations of the world will see that you are a people claimed by the Lord, and they will stand in awe of you.

The Lord will give you prosperity in the land He swore to your ancestors to give you, blessing you with many children, numerous livestock, and abundant crops.

The Lord will send rain at the proper time from His rich treasury in the heavens and will bless all the work you do. You will lend to many nations, but you will never need to borrow from them.

If you listen to these commands of the Lord your God that I am giving you today, and if you carefully obey them, the Lord will make you the head and not the tail, and you will always be on top and never at the bottom.

> *You must not turn away from any of the commands
> I am giving you today, nor follow after other gods and
> worship them* (My emphasis).

Now, I must try to explain a few things to you. What I just wrote was from the Old Testament. The children of Israel were under the law, we are under grace. They did not have Jesus, which means they did not have the Holy Spirit dwelling within them as we have. All they had was the law.

One Scripture comes to mind in the New Testament; Ephesians 3:20 (NLT)

> *Now all glory to God, who is able, through his mighty
> power at work within us, to accomplish infinitely more
> than we might ask or think* (My emphasis).

Can you see the difference between the Old Testament law and New Testament grace.

I noticed under the Old Testament that God called the Israelite's His people. I could be wrong, but I couldn't find where God called His people his children. They were called the children of Israel. But under the New Testament He considers us His children. What an honor!

I am so grateful we are not under the law but under grace.

If they did not obey the law the punishment for not obeying many of the laws was death.

If the punishment was not worthy of death, then the person who broke the law had to offer a sacrifice to cover his sin. Which animal was offered depended on which law was broken, and the sacrifice did not remove the sin, it only covered it.

For example, when a person cheated or stole from his neighbor they had to pay it back; sometimes up to seven times.

But we are under Grace; it says in 1 John 1:9 (NLT)

> *But if we confess our sins to Him, He is faithful and just to forgive us our sins and to cleanse us from all wickedness (Or unrighteousness), (My emphasis).*

In the New Testament when a person offends or steals from us we are to forgive them.

Oh, how glad I am to be under grace!

Yes, we should obey the commands of the Lord. Jesus said in John 14:15 (NLT).

> *"If you love me, obey my commandments"* (My emphasis).

He also said in Matthew 11:28-30 (NLT) Then Jesus said,

> *"come to Me, all of you who are weary and carry heavy burdens, and I will give you rest.*
>
> *"Take My yoke upon you. Let Me teach you, because I am humble and gentle at heart, and you will find rest for your souls.*
>
> *For My yoke is easy to bear, and My burden I give you is light"* (My emphasis).

Can we ever be separated from His love for us?

Paul wrote in Romans 8: 38, 39 (NLT)

> *"And I am convinced that nothing can ever separate us from God's love. Neither death nor life, neither angels nor demons, neither our fears for today nor our worries*

about tomorrow not even the powers of hell can separate us from God's love.

No power in the sky above or in Earth below, indeed nothing in all creation will ever be able to separate us from the love of God that is revealed in Christ Jesus our Lord "(My emphasis).

In 2 Peter 1:3,4 (NLT), God's word says;

by His divine power, God has given us everything we need for living a godly life. We have received all of this by coming to know Him, the one who called us to Himself by means of His marvelous glory and excellence.

And because of His glory and excellence, He has given us great and precious promises. These are the promises that enable you to share His divine nature and escape the world's corruption caused by human desires (My emphasis).

What does God's word say about the promises of God? You can find it in 2 Corinthians 1:20 (NLT).

For all of God's promises have been fulfilled in Christ with a resounding "yes!" And through Christ, our "Amen" (which means "yes") ascends to God for his glory (My emphasis).

I heard somewhere about a man whose last name was Storms he decided to count all the promises in the Bible. It took him a year and a half and he came up with the grand total of 8, 810 (7, 487 of them being promises made by God to humankind). And every one of them are yes and Amen in Christ.

CHAPTER 3

WE WILL NOT BE LEFT AS ORPHANS

King David prayed in Psalm 51:9-11 (NKJV).

> *Hide your face from my sins, and blot out my iniquities.*
> *Create in me a clean heart, O God, and renew a steadfast spirit within me.*
> *Do not cast me away from Your presence, and do not take Your Holy Spirit from me* (My emphasis).

In King David's day he was correct to pray this prayer. He did not have what we have today. Because, Jesus had not yet gone to the cross and made atonement for our sins.

We as new covenant believers have no need to pray this prayer and really shouldn't pray this prayer. We have what he was asking for, and God will not take it away from us; **EVER!**

The profit Ezekiel prophesied about the days we are living in when he prophesied in Ezekiel 36:26,27 (NLT).

And I will give you a new heart, and I will put a new spirit in you. I will take out your stony, stubborn heart and give you a tender, responsive heart.

And I will put My Spirit in you so that you will follow My decrees and be careful to obey My regulations (My emphasis).

This prophecy has been fulfilled.

Now we will go to the New Testament.

In the Gospel of John, as Jesus was preparing to go to the Father. He spoke to the disciples in; John 14:19-24 says (NLT)

"If you love me, obey my commandments.

And I will ask the Father, and He will give you another Advocate, who will never leave you.

He is the Holy Spirit, who leads into all truth. The world cannot receive Him, because it isn't looking for Him and doesn't recognize Him. But you know Him, because He is with you now and later will be in you.

No, I will not abandon you as orphans I will come to you.

Soon the world will no longer see Me, but you will see Me. Since I live, you also will live.

When I am raised to life again, you'll know that I am in My Father, and you are in Me, and I am in you.

Those who accept My commandments and obey them are the ones who love Me. And because they love Me, My Father will love them. And I will love them and will reveal Myself to each of them."

Judas (not Judas Iscariote) said to Him, "Lord, why are You going to reveal Yourself only to us and not to the world at large?"

Jesus replied, "all who love Me will do what I say. My Father will love them, and We will come and make our home with each of them.

"Anyone who doesn't love Me will not obey Me. And remember, My words are not My own. What I am telling you is from the Father who sent Me" (My emphasis).

Luke 24:49 (NLT) *Jesus said to the disciples; "and now I will send the Holy Spirit, just as My Father promised. For stay here in the city until the Holy Spirit comes and fills you with power from heaven"* (My emphasis).

The disciples could not do the work Jesus had called them to do unless they were **endued with power from on high,** and that power would come as the Holy Spirit was poured out upon them.

1 Corinthians 2:9-14 (NLT). But it was to us that God revealed these things by His Spirit. For His Spirit searches out everything and shows us God's deep secrets.

No one can know a person's thoughts except the person's own spirit, and no one can know God's thoughts except God's own Spirit.

And we have received God's Spirit (not the world's spirit), *so we can know the wonderful things God has freely given us.*

(Isaiah 64:4) This is what the Scripture means when it says, "no eye has seen, no ear has heard, and no mind has imagined what God has prepared for those who love Him.

When we tell you these things, we do not use words that come from human wisdom. Instead, we speak words given to us by the Spirit, using the Spirits words to explain spiritual truths.

But people who aren't spiritual can't receive these truths from God's Spirit. It all sounds foolish to them and they can't understand it, for only those who are spiritual can understand what the Spirit means.

CHAPTER 4

SPIRITUAL GIFTS AND THE FRUIT OF THE SPIRIT

There are other benefits from the Holy Spirit. One of them is the gifts of the Holy Spirit. 1 Corinthians 12:8-10 mentions nine of them. But first understand that these nine gifts fall into three divisions: the Gifts of Revelation, the Gifts of Inspiration and the Gifts of Power.

I have to apologize, because I could not find the source of the three divisions I am quoting. I found them in my research but could not determine the source. But they do match up with Scripture

GIFTS OF REVELATION

1:   The Word of Wisdom: A supernatural revelation, or insight into God's will and purpose, often given by the Spirit to solve difficult problems and situations.

2:    The Word of Knowledge: The Word of Knowledge is a supernatural revelation of God's knowledge or insight into God's mind, will or plan, to know things that could not be known by ourselves.

3:    Discerning of Spirits: This is a supernatural insight into the spirit definition of utterance realm to recognize their presence and know their plans.

GIFTS OF INSPIRATION

4:    Prophecy: prophecy is the supernatural speech in the native tongue. It is a miracle of God. Not conceived by human thought or reasoning. It's purpose is for edification, exhortation, and comfort.

5:    Divers Kinds of Tongues: The supernatural voice in other languages that are not known to the speaker.

6:    The Interpretation of Tongues: this ability is to interpret in the native tongue to a person or persons. Which is spoken in other languages not known by the one who interprets. It is supernaturally spoken by the Spirit.

GIFTS OF POWER

7:    Gift of Faith: this is a supernatural ability to believe God without any human doubt, unbelief, and rationalizations.

8:    The Gift of Healing: is the healing of all manner of sickness by the supernatural power of the Spirit of God, it is void of all human aid or medicine.

9:    The Gift of Miracles: A miracle is when God intervenes in the normal course of nature. It is temporary and goes against the naturally running of the universe. They are supernatural, going beyond what is natural. There is no natural explanation for these miracles.

There are also seven motivational gifts given in Romans 12:6-8 (NLT).

In his grace, God has given us different gifts for doing certain things well. So if God has given you the ability to prophesy, speak out with as much faith as God has given you.

If your gift is serving others, serve them well. If you are a teacher, teach well.

If your gift is to encourage others, be encouraging. If it is giving, give generously. If God has given you leader-ship ability, take the responsibility seriously. And if you have a gift of showing kindness to others, do it gladly (My emphasis).

FRUIT OF THE SPIRIT

"The Vines Complete Expository Dictionary defines the Fruit of the Spirit as; the character of the Lord being reproduced in them, namely, love, joy, peace, patience, kindness, goodness, faithfulness, gentleness, and self-control."

Again, what, or who, is our character to be modeled after? Of course, we know; as defined above. We are to model the character of our Lord Jesus. Reproducing these fruit or character traits and attributes in our lives. This can only be accomplished through the indwelling of the Holy Spirit.

As Christians our character or attributes should be a primary focus in our lives.

We are a beacon of light shining in this dark world for all to see. We want others to see our conduct in the way we live our lives so that they will want what we have.

I will list the fruit again. They are found In Galatians 5: 22, 23 (NLT).

> *But the Holy Spirit produces this kind of fruit in our lives: love, joy, peace, patience, kindness, goodness, faithfulness, gentleness, and self-control. There is no law against these things!* (My emphasis).

This is in contrast to the fruit produced by the flesh; our old sinful nature.

They are listed in Galatians 5:19-21 (NLT)

> *When you follow the desires of your sinful nature, the results are very clear; sexual immorality, impurity, lustful pleasures,*
> *idolatry, sorcery, hostility, quarreling, jealousy, out-bursts of anger, selfish ambition, dissension, division,*
> *envy, drunkenness, wild parties, and other sins like these. Let me tell you again, as I have before, that anyone living that sort of life will not inherit the kingdom of God* (My emphasis).

Although we are born again and have the indwelling of the Holy Spirit; we will not reproduce these fruit perfectly in our new

Christian walk. We have the fruit but won't have the training to express them the way we should. This training comes by renewing your mind with the word of God.

The more the mind is renewed and conformed to the image of Jesus, as mentioned in Romans 8:29 (NLT)

> *For God knew His people in advance, and He chose them to become like His Son, so that His Son would be the first-born among many brothers and sisters* (My emphasis).

If we are to **become** like His Son; this suggests that it is a process that occurs over time.

I have not come even close to fully modeling the character of Jesus or displaying these nine fruit perfectly in my daily walk.. But, at the same time I know I have the ability and the power dwelling within me. So, I try to do better every day. It takes work and diligence to accomplish this; calling on the strength of the Holy Spirit to check me when I am not behaving accordingly. I have noticed growth in this process of displaying these nine fruit in my daily walk. And I look forward to growing more like Jesus.

I am going to walk us through these nine characteristics, in the order they are listed in God's word, and see what the Bible says about each one. My hope is, it will help us love others as Jesus loves us.

LOVE

The word love here in the Greek is agape, in the New Testament it is usually the love of God for His Son and His people, and the love His people are to have for God, each other, and even enemies.

Wow! That's a tall order. I was doing okay, until I came to: and even enemies. As I began to study this out, I could see, this is exactly what Jesus wants us to do.

Luke 6:27-29 (NLT) says,

> *but to you who are willing to listen, I say, love your ene-mies! Do good to those who hate you.*

It doesn't stop there; verses 28 and 29 Jesus goes on to say,

> *bless those who curse you. Pray for those who hurt you.*

When Jesus hung on the cross the soldiers were gambling for his garment. Jesus said to the Father;

> *"forgive them, for they don't know what they are doing"*
> (Luke 23:34).

He was talking about them crucifying Him.

This love is an outward proof of the Holy Spirit's work in the life of the believer.

And that is remembering what Jesus taught repeatedly, like when he was asked, what are the greatest commandments?

He answered in Mark 12:30,31 (NLT).

> *And you must love the Lord your God with all your heart, all your soul, all your mind, and all your strength.*
>
> *The second is equally important: love your neighbor as yourself. No other commandment is greater than these* (My emphasis).

Luke 6:29 (NLT) *If someone slaps you on one cheek, offer the other cheek also. If someone demands your coat, offer your shirt also* (My emphasis).

God loved us when we were yet sinners. We are to love others in the same way.

Jesus said in John 13:34 (NLT)

So now I am giving you a new commandment: love each other. Just as I have loved you, you should love each other (My emphasis).

To love one another is a commandment. Not an option. 1 Corinthians 13 is sometimes called the love chapter. Here Paul writes in verses 1-7 (NLT)

If I could speak all the languages of the earth and of angels, but didn't love others, I would only be a noisy gong or a clanging symbol.

If I had the gift of prophecy and if I understood all of God's secret plans and possessed all knowledge, and if I had such faith that I could move mountains, but didn't love others, I would be nothing.

If I gave everything I have to the poor and even sacrifice my body, I could boast about it; but if I didn't love others, I would have gained nothing.

Love is patient and kind. Love is not jealous or boastful or proud or rude. It does not demand its own way. It is not irritable, and it keeps no record of being wronged.

It does not rejoice about injustice but rejoices when ever the truth wins out.

Love never gives up, never loses faith, is always hopeful, and endures through every circumstance (My emphasis).

In all these ways we are to treat other people who are not good to us, we don't have to like what they do to us, or the way they treat us, but we do have to love them. We are to bless and not curse. It is not when we feel like it or when they are doing what we ask. It's not just when they haven't wronged us. It's all the time.

Now, I have a question for you; "do you still want to be all in?" Because this is what it takes if you want everything God has for you.

That is what it means to walk in love and imitating Christ.

JOY

"According to Colorado University Rick Warren gave us this definition of joy: "joy is the settled assurance that God is in control of all the details of our lives, the quiet confidence that ultimately everything is going to be all right and a determined choice to praise God in every situation."

Joy in the Greek is chara it is closely related to charis, which means grace or a gift. Chara is a normal response to charis. We only have true joy because of God's grace.

Salvation should give us the greatest joy. Even in heaven when a sinner is saved all of heaven rejoices.

Luke 15:7 (NLT). In *the same way, there is more joy in heaven over one lost sinner who repents and returns to God then over ninety-nine others who are righteous and haven't strayed away!* (My emphasis).

John 15:11 (NLT). *I have told you these things so that you will be filled with My joy. Yes, your joy will overflow!* (My emphasis).

In the context of the above Scripture, John 15:11 Jesus is talking about the love of the Father and keeping Jesus's commandments.

Here is another Scripture speaking about the joy of God's presence.

Psalm 16:11 (NLT). *You will show me the way of life, granting me the joy of your presence and the pleasures of living with you for ever* (My emphasis).

Nehemiah 8:10 (NLT) says; *and Nehemiah continued, go and celebrate with a feast of rich foods and sweet drinks, and share gifts of food with people who have nothing prepared. This is a sacred day before our Lord. Don't be dejected and sad, for the joy of the Lord is your strength!* (My emphasis).

Psalm 30:5b (NLT) *weeping may last through the night, but joy comes with the morning.*

Philippians 4:4 (NLT) *always be full of joy in the Lord. I say it again rejoice!*

Romans 12:15 (NLT) *rejoice with them that do rejoice, and weep with them that weep* (My emphasis).

When I am filled with the joy of the Lord my strength is stronger and my faith is definitely increased.

PEACE

"It describes harmonious relationships between men, and between nations." As defined by the Vines Complete Expository Dictionary.

It is a supernatural peace that comes from the Holy Spirit (As all the fruit do). An inner knowing that everything is going to be all right. Where anxieties and worries are overcome with the peace of God.

When I am anxious I remind myself that God is in control. He loves me, He is for me and he promised to keep me in perfect peace when my mind is stayed on Him. A knowing that all things work for good.

> Isaiah 26:3 (NLT) *You'll keep in perfect peace all who trust in You, all whose thoughts are fixed on You!*

> Philippians 4:6, 7 (NLT) *Don't worry about anything; instead, pray about everything. Tell God what you need, and thank Him for all He has done.*
> *Then you will experience God's peace, which exceeds anything we can understand. His peace will guard your hearts and minds as you live in Christ Jesus.*

> Psalm 29:11 (NLT) *The Lord gives His people strength. The Lord blesses them with peace* (My emphasis).

PATIENCE

I have made being patient a goal in my life. I say this because of what I've read in the book of James.

> James 1:4 (NKJV) *But let patience have its perfect work, that you may be perfect and complete, lacking nothing* (My emphasis).

I want to be perfect and complete as possible and for sure I do not want to lack anything. On my own this is impossible, but I am not on my own; I have the Holy Spirit guiding and leading me into all truth.

We need patience in so many areas of our lives; with our children, in our workplace, in the store checkout line, driving in traffic and many other areas.

I know I must be growing in patience because both of my best friends tell me I am the most patient person they have ever known. One of them says, "you don't freak out about anything!" Praise God! The fruit of the Spirit in my life is becoming noticed by others.

You may not realize it but others are watching you; especially unbelievers. The outward proof of these character traits is a witness to them. Some of them will want what you have, and who knows; you may lead them to Christ.

Below are a few scriptures about the importance of patience.

> Ephesians 4:2 (NLT) *Always be humble and gentle. Be patient with each other, making allowance for each other's faults because of your love.*

James 5:7 (NLT) *Dear brothers and sisters, be patient as you wait for the Lord's return. Consider the farmers who patiently wait for the rains in the fall and in the spring. They eagerly look for the valuable harvest to ripen* (My emphasis).

One thing I believe James is saying here is; wait patiently and eagerly for what God has promised you. Because, it is coming.

Colossians 3:12 (NLT) *Since God chose you to be the holy people He loves, you must clothe yourselves with tenderhearted mercy, kindness, humility, gentleness, and patience.*

Romans 12:12 (NLT). Paul speaking of gifts and how to behave in life.
Rejoice in our confident hope. Be patient in trouble, and keep on praying.

Romans 15:4, 5 (NLT). *Such things were written in the Scriptures long ago to teach us. And the Scriptures give us hope and encouragement as we wait patiently for God's promises to be fulfilled.*
May God, who gives this patience and encouragement, help you live in complete harmony with each other, as is fitting for followers of Christ Jesus.

1 Corinthians 13:4 (NLT) *Love is patient and kind. Love is not jealous or boastful or proud.*

Ecclesiastics 7:8 (NKJV). *The end of a thing is better than its beginning: the patient in spirit is better than the proud in spirit* (My emphasis).

KINDNESS

As believers in Christ we are to be kind and show kindness to everyone, in every situation.

We are to be different from the ways most of the people of this world conduct themselves.

Many of them believe it is right and natural to be and say what Ephesians 4: 31,32 (NLT) tells us to get rid of;

get rid of all bitterness, rage, anger, harsh words, and slander, as well as all types of evil behavior.

Instead, be kind to each other, tenderhearted, forgiving one another, just as God through Christ has forgiven you.

If someone says something to them in rage or anger and uses harsh words, they believe that it's proper to respond in the same way.

I will give you a recent example from my own life that describes that kind of response from Ephesians 4:31.

I had just pulled out a coffee shop drive thru and I became distracted putting my change in my pocket. I thought I had stopped rolling, the next thing I knew, I rolled right into a vehicle.

The driver jumped out of his vehicle and began yelling curse words at me! I calmly got out of my vehicle and softly said to the man; "Sir, please forgive me." Immediately he stopped cursing and became very kind.

I had just witnessed what Proverb 15:1 (NKJV) says;

> *a soft answer turns away wrath, but a harsh word stirs up*
> *anger* (My emphasis).

Instead of yelling back, I responded like Proverb 15:1 and Ephesians 4:32 tells us to respond.

GOODNESS

Goodness and kindness are very similar, but yet very distinct. They have to be because they are two separate distinct Fruit of the Spirit.

The way I look at the two is; that kindness is a byproduct of goodness, especially when it comes to the goodness (righteousness) of God. Where God's goodness is present; kindness is the result.

We can see God's goodness in many ways; the sun rises every day, the rain waters the earth, the seasons come and go on time and God's promises are yes and Amen.

> Psalm 31:19 (NLT) *How great is the goodness You have*
> *stored up for those who fear You. You lavish it on those*
> *who come to You for protection, blessing them before the*
> *watching world.*

> James 1:17 (NLT) *Whatever is good and perfect comes*
> *down to us from God our Father, Who created all the*
> *lights in the heavens. He never changes or casts a shifting*
> *shadow.*

Romans 8:28 (NLT) *And we know that God causes everything to work together for the good of those who love God and are called according to His purpose for them.*

Psalm 27:13 (NLT) *Yet I am confident I will see the Lord's goodness while I am here in the land of the living.*

FAITHFULNESS

The first thing I think of, or should I say, first one, is God and His faithfulness to me; even when I am not faithful to Him. He remains faithful to me.

If our desire is to be like Jesus, then we need to remain faithful, to Him first, then, in our close relationships. Especially, if were married, faithfulness to our spouses results in fidelity to them. Then our friends. Then, let that spillover to others that we come into contact with during our every day walk. Even if they're only there for a short time.

God is one hundred percent faithful to His Word one hundred percent of the time; we need to be the same way.

Personally, I have not had much of a problem being faithful to my word. When I was growing up I was taught that my word is my bond. Today, everyone wants a contract to bind us to our word; even when we may borrow from a friend, some of them will want a Personal Note binding us to pay back the loan. When I was much younger our word was a binding contract; we would shake hands and that was the end of it, it was a done deal.

2 Timothy 2:13 (NLT) *If we are unfaithful, He remains faithful, for He cannot deny Himself.*

2 Thessalonians 3:3 (NLT*) But the Lord is faithful; he will strengthen you and guard you from the evil one.*

Proverbs 20:6 (NKJV) *Most men will proclaim each his own goodness, but who can find a faithful man?*

Proverbs 2:8 (NLT) *He guards the paths of the just and protects those who are faithful to Him.*

1 Corinthians 1:9 (NLT) *God will do this, for He is faithful to do what He says, and He has invited you into partnership with His Son, Jesus Christ our Lord.*

1 Corinthians 4:2(NLT) *Now, a person who is put in charge as a manager must be faithful* (My emphasis).

If you research you will find many more scriptures like these on faithfulness.

GENTLENESS

"According to Grand Canyon University: gentleness **comes from a state of humility.** Therefore, someone who lacks gentleness is often prideful and easily angered, or feels the need for revenge. In order to be gentle, we must not view ourselves as better than someone else."

As a Marine I was proud, you know the saying; "The Few the Proud the Marines." When I came home from serving my nation; I believed that I had to take control of everything and everyone in my life. Especially family, finances, and anyone else who opposed me.

This was not the Corps fault! It was my perception.

So, I was not a humble or gentle civilian. You may have also heard "you can take the man out of the Corps but you can't take the Corps out of the man." That last statement is so very true. Even though I'm a Christian now and do my best to walk in humility; I still have the Corps in me,but today it has more of a positive effect, then a negative effect.

The price of becoming humble was very high; it cost my family dearly, especially my wife and children, I changed the course of a lot of lives. All due to a horrific tragedy caused by schizophrenia. This disease did nothing but feed my pride. I wish my humility could've came a lot sooner, at a much cheaper price. I was blinded, tricked by the enemy and a devastating disease that I didn't even know I had. (You can read about this tragedy in my first book I mentioned in the introduction).

Titus 3:2 (NLT) *They must not slander anyone and must avoid quarreling. Instead, they should be gentle and show true humility to everyone.* Here Titus is telling believers to submit to the powers that be; such as the government and to be ready always to do good (Paraphrased).

Ephesians 4:2 (NLT) *Always be humble and gentle. Be patient with each other, making allowance for each other's faults because of your love.*

Matthew 11:29 (NLT) *Take my yoke upon you. Let me teach you, because I am humble and gentle at heart, and you will find rest for your souls.*

Colossians 3:12 (NLT) *Since God chose you to be the holy people he loves, you must clothe yourselves with tenderhearted mercy, kindness, humility, gentleness, and patience.*

2 Corinthians 10:1 (NLT) *Now I, Paul, appeal to you with the gentleness and kindness of Christ though I realize you think I am timid in person and bold only when I write from far away.*

The context of this verse is Paul begging the Corinthian church that when he sees them he won't have to be bold with those in the church that think he acts from human motives (Paraphrased).

1 Timothy 3:3 (NLT). *He must not be a heavy drinker or be violent. He must be gentle, not quarrelsome, and not love money* (My emphasis). The context of this verse is Paul telling his spiritual son, Timothy, the qualifications of a bishop (Paraphrased).

SELF-CONTROL

"Oxford Languages defines self-control as the ability to control one's self, in particular one's emotions and desires or the expression of them in one's behavior, especially in difficult situations."

Self-control is the last character trait listed in the Fruit of the Spirit. The definition above speaks of two different types of self-control; the first is one's emotions. Your emotions, at least for me, have a very wide range, such as, the emotion of being happy, being sad, being angry. The expression of these emotions may be low key or very extreme. Have you ever been hysterically laughing about something very funny that you had no self-control to stop. Or maybe so sad that you could not stop sobbing. Or so angry that you wanted to strike out at something or someone.

The more difficult the situation, whether good or bad, funny or sad will fluctuate, depending on how you allow yourself to express these emotions and how much self-control you have over them.

The other one defined by Oxford languages is the ability to control our desires. Again, the range or difficulty of controlling our desires will vary depending on our self-control over them.

Say I have an addiction to nicotine, which I do, there are days when my self-control to not smoke varies a lot due to the atmosphere I am in. I have been in the hospital four days and not smoked and experienced very little desire. As soon as I got out of the hospital, within minutes I was lighting up a cigarette (Crazy huh).

Addictions are what the Bible calls strongholds, of course there are others.

The stronghold of smoking, at that time, had more control over me than I had over it.

Here are some scriptures about self-control.

> 1 Corinthians 9:27 (NLT) *I discipline my body like an athlete, training it to do what it should. Otherwise, I fear that after preaching to others I myself might be disqualified*

(I personally need to meditate on this scripture).

> 1 Corinthians 10:13 (NLT) *The temptations in your life are no different from what others experience. And God is faithful. He will not allow the temptation to be more*

*than you can stand. When you are tempted, he will show
you a way out so that you can endure.*

(Boy! Those two scriptures are ministering to me, how about you?).

2 Peter 1:5 (NLT). *And in view of all this, make every
effort to respond to God's promises. Supplement your faith
with a generous provision of moral excellence, and moral
excellence with knowledge,
    And knowledge with self-control, and self-control
with patient endurance, and patient endurance with
godliness*

These last two scriptures are in the context of receiving God's promises, so that we may be partakers of his divine nature.

The more you practice self-control the more you are in obedience to God; in respect to walking in love. Which takes, at times, much self-control.

CHAPTER 5

HOPE

First; we must understand, that HOPE is future tense; it is the pre-requisite for faith. You cannot have faith without first having HOPE.

Second; HOPE has no substance; faith brings substance to our HOPE. Hebrews 11:1 (NLT) says;

> *Faith is the confidence that what we HOPE for will actually happen; it gives us assurance about things we cannot see* (My Emphasis).

HOPE is an anchor of our soul; then just where is it anchored? The answer is found in Hebrews 6:19 (NLT); says:

> *This HOPE is a strong and trustworthy anchor for our souls. It leads us through the curtain and into God's inner sanctuary* (My Emphasis).

What does it mean through the curtain? It means the very throne room of God; We are anchored in and to Jesus!

A well-known Scripture is Romans 4:18 (KJV); speaking of Abraham;

> *Who against HOPE believed in HOPE, that he might become the father of many nations, according to that which was spoken. So shall thy seed be* (My Emphasis).

Why was it against HOPE that he believed in HOPE? God told Abraham, now almost an hundred years old, that he was going to have a son: **that is against HOPE!** But, he mixed it with faith and the promise came to pass.

> Proverbs 13:12 (NLT). It says; *HOPE deferred makes the heart sick, but a dream fulfilled is a tree of life* (Emphasis added).

The Bible says there are three things that eternally abide, they are listed in

> 1 Corinthians 13:13 (NLT); *three things will last forever faith, HOPE, and love and the greatest of these is love* (My Emphasis).

HOPE is listed as one of the three things that will eternally abide.

So, how do we obtain this HOPE, I'm letting you know, you may not like the answer. The answer is found in Romans 5:3-5 (NLT*)*.

We can rejoice, too, when we run into problems and tri-als, for we know that they help us develop endurance. And endurance develops strength of character, and character strengthens our confident HOPE of salvation. And this HOPE will not lead to disappointment. (My Emphasis).

The Apostle Paul wrote in Colossians 1:20-23 (NLT)

and through him God reconciled everything to himself. He made peace with everything in heaven and on earth by means of Christ's blood on the cross.

This includes you who were once far away from God. You were his enemies, separated from him by your evil thoughts and actions. Yet now he has reconciled you to himself through the death of Christ in his physical body. As a result, he has brought you into his own presence, and you are holy and blameless as you stand before him without a single fault.

But you must continue to believe this truth and stand firmly in it. Don't drift away from the assurance you received when you heard the Good News. The Good News has been preached all over the world, and I, Paul, have been appointed as God's servant to proclaim it. (My emphasis).

Put your hope in Christ.

The word HOPE appears 130 times in the Bible. These were just a few times, but I believe these are indispensable for our Christian walk.

I will close with this final Scripture:

Ps. 131, *Let Israel* (that's us) *HOPE in the Lord from henceforth and for ever.* (My Emphasis).

CHAPTER 6

FAITH

For some reason it took me a very long time to understand how faith works. So I decided to research it and seek understanding from the Holy Spirit.

Faith is a very powerful supernatural force. It has the ability to bring into reality something that does not exist, and cause it to exist. It also has the ability to remove problems, no matter how big they may be.

Remember I wrote earlier, that the Christian walk is a process.

Well for me, my faith increasing has been a process too. When I first began testing the realm of faith, the more I believed that I would receive what I was asking for, the more I started to receive what I was asking for. As long as I was asking for something that God's Word says I could have, and if it's a promise in God's Word, then there is no reason for doubt or unbelief.

Belief and faith go hand-in-hand. You can't have true faith for something if you don't believe, believe what? That you're going to receive that something. When you truly believe you're going to receive what you asked for, that is your **faith** working.

Jesus said in Mark 11:23 (NKJV)

> *For assuredly, I say to you, whoever says to this mountain, be removed and be cast into the sea, and does not doubt in his heart, but believes that those things he says will be done, he will have whatever he says* (My emphasis).

Do you understand the magnitude of that Scripture.

Remember, I wrote, Scripture confirms Scripture with Scripture. Jesus said in the very next verse; Mark 11:24 (NLT)

> *I tell you, you can pray for anything, and if you believe that you received it, it will be yours* (My emphasis).

Confirming verse 23.

> Hebrews 11:1 gives us the definition of faith; it says (NLT) *Faith is the confidence that what we hope for will actually happen; it gives us assurance about things we cannot see* (My emphasis).

I like the Amplified Classic Version of this Scripture, which says;

> *Now faith is the assurance (the confirmation, the title deed) of the things [we] hope for, being a proof of things [we] do not see and the conviction of their reality [faith perceiving as real fact what is not yet revealed to the senses]* (My emphasis).

There are a couple conditions that have to be put in place to receive this kind of mountain moving faith. 1: you have to believe what you're asking for will come into being. 2: you cannot doubt, no matter what. No matter how long it takes in the natural. Unbelief and doubt will stop a blessing in its tracks!

James said a couple of things that relate to this. James 1:3-4 (NKJV)

> *Knowing that the testing of your faith produces patience. But let patience have its perfect work, that you may be perfect and complete, lacking nothing* (My emphasis).

Another thing I've learned over time is that faith must have a corresponding action. Such as helping someone with a physical need, or sowing a seed, usually a financial seed, targeting that seed for what you are believing for. I've learned helping someone else with getting their need met will get God's attention. God has no problem giving you what you ask for. But he's also watching what your motive is for that blessing.

> James said in James 4:1-3 (NLT). *What is causing your quarrels and fights among you? Don't they come from the evil desires at war within you? You want what you don't have, so you scheme and kill to get it. You are jealous of what others have, but you can't get it, so you fight and wage war to take it away from them. Yet you don't have what you want because you don't ask God for it. And even when you ask, you don't get it because your motives are all wrong; you want only what will give you pleasure* (My emphasis).

Those are some powerful words, but with many people they are true.

Let's talk some more about faith.

We'll talk about the Hall of faith as listed in Hebrews 11. We will start in verse two; (NLT).

Through their faith, the people in days of old earned a good reputation.

By faith we understand that the entire universe was formed at God's command, that what we now see did not come from anything that can be seen.

It was by faith that Abel brought a more acceptable offering to God than Cain did. Abel's offering gave evidence that he was a righteous man, and God showed His approval of his gifts. Although Abel is long dead, he still speaks to us by the example of faith.

It was by faith that Enoch was taken up to heaven without dying, he disappeared, because God took him. For before he was taken out, he was known as a person who pleased God.

And it is impossible to please God without faith. Anyone who wants to come to Him must believe that God exists and that He rewards those who sincerely seek Him.

It was by faith that Noah built a large boat to save his family from the flood. He obeyed God, who warned him about things that had never happened before. By his faith Noah condemned the world and became heir of the righteousness which is according to faith.

It was by faith Abraham obeyed when God called him to leave home and go to another land that God would give them as his inheritance. He went without knowing where he was going.

And even when he reached the land God promised him, he lived there by faith for he was like a foreigner, living in tents. And so did Isaac and Jacob, who inherited the same promise.

Abraham was confidently looking forward to a city with eternal foundations, a city designed and built by God.

Through faith also Sarah herself also received strength to conceive seed, and was able to have a child, though she was barren and was too old. She believed that God would keep his promise.

And so a whole nation came from this one man who was as good as dead. A nation with so many people that, like the stars in the sky and the sand on the seashore, there is no way to count them.

All these people died still believing what God had promised them. They did not receive what was promised, but they saw it all from a distance and welcomed it. They agreed that they were foreigners and nomads here on earth.

Obviously people who say such things are looking forward to a country they can call their own.

If they longed for the country they came from, they could've gone back.

But they were looking for a better place, a heavenly homeland. That is why God is not ashamed to be called their God, for he has prepared a city for them.

It was by faith that Abraham offered Isaac as a sacrifice when God was testing him. Abraham, who had received God's promises, was ready to sacrifice his only son, Isaac,

even though God had told him, Isaac is the son through whom your descendants will be counted.

Abraham reasoned that if Isaac died, God was able to bring him back to life again. And in a sense, Abraham did receive his son back from the dead.

It was by faith that Isaac promised blessings for the future of his sons, Jacob and Esau.

It was by faith that Jacob, when he was old and dying, blessed each of Joseph's sons and bowed in worship as he leaned on his staff.

It was by faith that Joseph, when he was about to die, said confidently that the people of Israel would leave Egypt. He commanded them to take his bones with them when they left.

It was by faith that Moses' parents hid him for three months when he was born. They saw that God had given them an unusual child, and they were not afraid to disobey the king's command.

It was by faith that Moses, when he grew up, refused to be called the son of Pharaoh's daughter.

He chose to share the oppression of God's people instead of enjoying the fleeting pleasures of sin.

He thought it was better to suffer for the sake of Christ than to own the treasures of Egypt, for he was looking ahead to his great reward.

It was by faith that Moses left the land of Egypt, not fearing the king's anger. He kept right on going because he kept his eyes on the one who was invisible.

It was by faith that Moses commanded the people of Israel to keep the Passover and to sprinkle blood on the doorposts so that the angel of death would not kill their firstborn sons.

It was by faith that the people of Israel went right through the Red Sea as though they were on dry ground. But when the Egyptians tried to follow, they were all drowned.

It was by faith that the people of Israel marched around Jericho for seven days, and the walls came crashing down.

It was by faith that Rahab the prostitute was not destroyed with the people in her city who refused to obey God. For she had given a friendly welcome to the spies.

How much more do I need to say? It would take too long to recount the stories of the faith of Gideon, Barak, Sampson, Jephthah, David, Samuel, and all the prophets.

By faith these people overthrew kingdoms, ruled with justice, and received what God had promised them. They shut the mouths of lions,

quenched the flames of fire, and escaped death by the edge of the sword. Their weakness was turned to strength. They became strong in battle and put whole armies to flight.

Women received their loved ones back again from death. But others were tortured, refusing to turn from God in order to be set free. They placed their hope in a better life after the resurrection.

Some were jeered at, and their backs were cut open with whips. Others were chained in prisons.

Some died by stoning, some were sawed in half and others were killed with the sword. Some went about wearing skins of sheep and goats destitute and oppressed and mistreated.

They were too good for this world, wandering over deserts and mountains, hiding in caves and holes in the ground.

All these people earned a good reputation because of their faith, yet none of them, received all that God had promised.

For God had something better in mind for us, so that they would not reach perfection without us (My emphasis).

I have just wrote all of Hebrews chapter 11 minus verse one, why did I do this? I did it to show you how important faith is. Two things to remember; faith is the power of God, and fear is the power of the enemy. It all depends on how you're going to respond. Respond in faith; come out victorious; respond in fear and come out defeated.

Paul wrote in Romans 3:27 (NLT)

Can we boast, then, that we have done anything to be accepted by God? No, because our acquittal is not based on obeying the law. It is based on faith (My emphasis).

Faith is a law, like any of the laws of the universe. It works first time and every time if you work it, if you believe.

Faith is not a feeling, on the contrary, it is a choice that we make to believe no matter what comes against us. After you make the choice to stay in faith, no matter what, the next step is patience. I guess you can say; patience is the foundation of faith. It holds it up under any circumstance. If you are believing for a healing, but the symptoms are getting worse, don't throw in the towel. If you're having these passing thoughts that your faith is not working; remember this, having passing thoughts does not mean you're wavering in your faith. It's just a tactic of the enemy to try to stop you from your blessing. Keep believing, keep trusting, stay in the Spirit of Victory.

The closer you come to getting your answer, the greater the fight of faith is going to be. The enemy knows if he can get you out of patience and faith, through your thought life, he can keep you from your answer.

The mind is the control center of our thoughts and beliefs. If the enemy can get control of your mind, he can take control of you. Everything goes through the mind first. That's why we walk by faith and not by sight. If you are leaning on your own understanding then you are no longer walking by faith, but by sight.

There are different levels of fear as well as different levels of faith. The fear may start out at a low-level, but if you let it go unchecked it can turn into panic and despair. Once that happens you have to gird up your faith and fight the good fight of faith. You have to have the same level of faith our father Abraham had. He stayed in faith for 20 years, believing God, that what He said He was able to do.

This is where patience comes in. You may say you don't have patience, but that's not true, if you are a born-again believer you have patience; because it's one of the fruit of the spirit, that has been put inside you. You need to look inside and bring it out, because it's in their.

God said; "He had given us everything that pertains to life and godliness", the key word here is, everything. So when fear comes knocking at your door, answer it with faith because faith works, if you work it.

There are some battles you might get through with a little faith, but there are some where we need the faith of God. When the doctor tells you, "you have one year to live"; a little faith is not going to get you over. If you let the fear of death kick in, you'll start losing the battle for your healing.

You have to tell yourself what Paul said; "to live is Christ, to die is gain." If you get to that level of faith, it is going to be hard for you to be defeated.

James wrote in James 1:2-4. (NLT).

> *Dear brothers and sisters, when troubles come your way, consider it an opportunity for great joy.*
>
> *For you know that when your faith is tested, your endurance has a chance to grow.*
>
> *So let it grow, for when your endurance is fully developed, you will be perfect and complete needing nothing.*

If you think for one minute, that your faith isn't going to be tested, then you are dearly mistaken. God is not going to give you something that you're not ready to receive. You may think you're ready, but believe me God knows. He knows what you want it for, and what you plan to do with it. He knows your thoughts before you think them.

It's not that he doesn't want to give you the desires of your heart, on the contrary, he just wants you to be ready when he does give it to you.

I waited 30 years for something that I wanted. I waited, and waited, and waited. I thought it was a dead issue. But then, one day out of nowhere I received what I had been asking for. But it wasn't until I was ready to receive it.

Like many of us I did not come from money, and I had a poverty mindset. So every time I got a little money I wasn't satisfied until I spent it. Then I was back to the same place I was before the money came.

God had to remove that poverty mindset. and to learn that the money he gives me is not to spend on my own desires only but to put others first. When I made up my mind to do this, everything changed; for the better. Now I have enough for myself and for others.

If you see someone in a dire need, whether you know them or not, and you have the means to help them, please help them. This will make them more receptive to receive the good word you have about the gospel of Jesus Christ. Telling them about the gospel and at the same time not helping them in their need will only close their heart to hear you.

We have to remember that we are blessed so that we could be a blessing. If you do these things you will never lack for any good thing.

Always remember, Jesus came to give us life and life more abundantly. But He said, seek first the kingdom of God and His righteousness and all these other things will be added to you. He also said, give and it shall be given back to you, pressed down, shaken together, and running over, shall men give into your bosom. It doesn't say God will give it to you, it says others will give it to you.

God will cause people to want to help you, and give you what you need. It's just a matter of following the directions in His word. They work first time and every time, without fail. God is faithful, if He said it He will do it.

You can actually start a cycle of giving and receiving in your life.

In the last chapter of this book I will be writing about giving.

James 1:12-15 (NLT) *Blessed is the man who endures temptation; for when he has been approved, he will receive the crown of life which the Lord has promised to those who love him.*

And remember, when you are being tempted, do not say, God is tempting me. God is never tempted to do wrong, and He never tempts anyone else.

Temptation comes from our own desires, which entice us and drag us away.

These desires give birth to sinful actions. And when sin is allowed to grow, it gives birth to death (My emphasis).

1 Timothy 6:10 (NLT) *For the love of money is the root of all kinds of evil. And some people, craving money, have wandered from the true faith and pierced themselves with many sorrows* (My emphasis).

Money is not the root of all evil, the **LOVE** of money is. Money is neither good nor bad it's neutral, its what you do with it that's good or bad.

Philippians 2:3, 4 (NLT). *Don't be selfish; don't try to impress others. Be humble, thinking of others as better than yourselves.*

Don't look out only for your own interests, but take an interest in others, too (My emphasis).

Remember; fear and faith cannot coexist in the same place. You're either in fear or your in faith. And also remember, fear and faith is a choice. So choose faith. They are not feelings, feelings can change at any moment depending on the circumstances. But if you make the choice to stay in faith and gird it up with patience, you can win the battle.

CHAPTER 7

FEAR

We have to come to a place of understanding, fear is a tactic of the enemy to get us out of faith.

The Bible is full of verses that tell us to stay in faith and to not fear. It's all a matter of perspective, either you believe God or you believe the enemy. Just a matter of perspective.

When I was in the Marine Corps we were told the story about a platoon of Marines surrounded by the enemy. A private went to the Gunnery Sgt. and said, "Sgt., the enemy is in front of us, in our rear, on our left flank and on our right flank, what shall we do!"

The gunnery Sgt. looked at him and said, "good, they can't get away from us now!"

A matter of perspective, one saw defeat, the others saw victory.

The Bible has a similar story; the Syrian army had surrounded Elisah's house. When his servant woke up, he looked outside and saw thousands of Syrians. He ran to Elisha and said, "Master how shall we do!" Elisah said, "there are more that are for us than are against us!" He prayed to God and asked, "Lord, open his eyes." His servant looked outside again, this time he saw thousands of warring angels and chariots of fire surrounding Elisah's house. A matter of perspective.

Remember this; if God chooses to fight a battle he will never ever lose!

The Psalms are full of scriptures about trust and faith. Psalm 91:7 (NLT)

Though a thousand fall at your side, though 10,000 are dying around you, these evils will not touch you (My emphasis).

Then there is this story of Shadrach, Meshach and Abednego in Daniel 3: 16-26 (NLT).

Shadrach, Meshack, and Abednego replied, "oh Nebuchadnezzar, we do not need to defend ourselves before you.

If we are thrown into the blazing furnace, the God whom we serve is able to save us. He will rescue us from your power, your Majesty.

But even if He doesn't, we want to make it clear to you, your Majesty, that we will never serve your gods or worship the gold statue you have set up.

Then Nebuchadnezzar was full of fury, and the expression on his face changed toward Shadrach, Meshack, and Abednego. He spoke and commanded that they heat the furnace seven times more than it was usually heated.

Then he ordered some of the strongest men of his army to bind Shadrach, Meshack, and Abednego and through them into the blazing furnace.

So they tied them up and threw them into the furnace, fully dressed in their pants, turbines, robes, and other governments.

And because the king, in his anger, had demanded such a hot fire in the furnace, the flames killed the soldiers as they through the three men in.

So Shadrach, Meshack, Abednego securely tied, fell into the roaring flames.

But suddenly, Nebuchadnezzar jumped up in amazement and exclaimed to his advisors, "didn't we tie up three men and throw them into the furnace?" "Yes, your Majesty, we certainly did," they replied.

"Look! Nebuchadnezzar shouted I see four men, unbound, walking around in the fire unharmed! And the fourth looks like a God!"

Then Nebuchadnezzar came as close as he could to the door of the flaming furnace and shouted: "Shadrach, Meshack, and Abednego, servants of the most high God, come out! Come here!" So Shadrach, Meshack, and Abednego, stepped out the fire.

Then the high officers, officials, governors, and advisors crowding around them and saw that the fire had not touched them. Not a hair on their heads was singed, and their cloths were not scorched. They didn't even smell of smoke!

Then Nebuchadnezzar spake, and said, "Blessed be the God of Shadrach, Meshack, and Abednego, who has sent His angel, and delivered His servants that trusted in Him, and have changed the king;s word, and yielding their bodies, that they may not serve or worship any God except their own God!

Therefore, I make this decree: "if any people, whatever their race or nation or language, speak a word against the God of Shadrach, Meshack, and Abednego, they will be torn limb from limb and their houses will be turned into heaps of rubble. There is no other God who can rescue like this!"

Then the king promoted Shadrach, Meshack, and Abednego in the province of Babylon. (My emphasis).

Just a matter of perspective.

Then there is the story of Daniel, in Daniel 6:22 where he was thrown into a den of hungry lions, and the angel of the Lord shut the mouths of the lions and Daniel laid down and slept the night. A matter of perspective. Faith over fear will get you through every time.

In the book of Proverbs chapter 29:25 (NLT)

Fearing people is a dangerous trap, but trusting the Lord means safety.

In Joshua 1:9 (NLT) *This is my command; "be strong and courageous! Do not be afraid or discouraged. For the Lord your God is with you wherever you go"*

Psalm 23:4 (NLT) *"Even when I walk through the darkest valley, I will not be afraid, for You are close beside me. Your rod and Your staff protect and comfort me."*

Psalms 27:1 (NLT) *A Psalm of David. "The Lord is my light and my salvation so why should I be afraid? The*

Lord is my fortress, protecting me from danger, so why should I tremble?"

Psalms 34:4-8(NLT) "I prayed to the Lord, and he answered me.

He freed me from all my fears. Those who look to him for help will be radiant with joy, no shadow of shame will darken their faces. In my desperation I prayed, and the Lord listened, he saved me from all my troubles. For the angel of the Lord is a guard; he surrounds and defends all who fear Him. Taste and see that the Lord is good, oh, the joys of those who take refuge in him!"

Psalms 46:1-3 (NLT) "God is our refuge and strength, always ready to help in times of trouble. So we will not fear when earthquakes come and the mountains crumble into the sea. Let the oceans roar and foam. Let the mountains tremble as the waters serge!"

Psalms 56:3-7 (NLT) "Oh God!, have mercy on me, for people are hounding me. My foes attack me all day long. I am constantly hounded by those who slandered me, and many are boldly attacking me. But when I am afraid, I will put my trust in you, I praise God for what he has promised. I trust in God so why should I be afraid? What can mere mortals do to me? They are always twisting what I say, they spend their days plotting to harm me. They come together to spy on me, watching my every step, eager to kill me. Don't let them get away with their wickedness; in your anger, oh God, bring them down."

Psalms 91:4-5 (NLT) *He will cover you with his feathers. He will shelter you with his wings. His faithful promises are your armor and protection. Do not be afraid of the terrors of the night, nor the arrow, that flies in the day.*

Psalms 107:28-30 (NLT) *"Lord help!" They cried in their troubles, and he saved them from their distress. He calmed the storm to a whisper and stilled the waves. What a blessing was that stillness, as he brought them safely into harbor!*

Psalms 112:6-8 (NLT) *Such people will not be overcome by evil. Those who are righteous will be long remembered. They do not fear bad news; they confidently trust the Lord to care for them. They are confident and fearless and can face their foes triumphantly.*

Isaiah 41:8-10 (NLT) *But as for you, Israel my servant, Jacob my chosen one, descended from Abraham my friend, I have called you back from the ends of the earth saying. You are my servant for I have chosen you and will not throw you away. Don't be afraid, for I am with you, don't be discouraged, for I am your God, I will strengthen you and help you. I will hold you up with my victorious right hand* (My emphasis).

And there is many more scriptures. Do you think that God is trying to tell us not to be afraid?

CHAPTER 8

OUR SPIRITUAL ARMOR

2 Peter 1:3 (NLT) *By his divine power, God has given us everything we need for living a godly life. We have received all of this by coming to know him, the one who called us to himself by means of his marvelous glory and excellence* (My emphasis).

One of the things God gave us was spiritual weapons. We will now talk about that.

Paul says in 2 Corinthians 10:4 (NLT)

We use God's mighty weapons, not worldly weapons, to knock down the strongholds of human reasoning and to destroy false arguments (My emphasis).

Paul wanted to explain to us these weapons that are spiritual not carnal. He wanted to relate to something we could understand. He came up with the idea of the Roman soldiers armor.

Paul was in prison many times, and most of those times he was chained to a Roman guard. He couldn't help but notice the soldiers armor. The Roman soldier has seven weapons. Six are listed in Ephesians 6:12-17. But there are seven weapons of the Roman soldier. The seventh weapon is listed in Ephesians 6:18.

Ephesians 6:12 -17

Like the weapons of the Roman soldier our spiritual weapons are both offensive and defensive.

Paul said in Ephesians 6:13. (NLT)

herefore, put on every piece of God's armor so you will be able to resist the enemy in the time of evil. Then after the battle you'll still be standing firm (My emphasis).

The first spiritual weapon we have is the loin belt of truth.

Loin belt of truth: the Roman soldiers loin belt was the most important weapon he had.

His loin belt helped him keep his breast plate in place. His shield was also clipped to his loin belt. His sword was also attached to his loin belt. Another words it held everything in place.

In the spiritual sense our loin belt is the Word of God. The Word of God is what holds all of our other spiritual weapons in place. The most important weapon is what is inside a man. If you don't carrying this weapon inside you on a daily basis, when you come into a battle you'll start to fall apart. If you don't know the Word of God you will be defeated every time!

Without this weapon you will spiritually begin to fall apart and your other weapons will not be able to do their job as they are intended to do.

The breastplate of righteousness: Roman soldiers breastplate protected his vital organs; in a sense it is the same way with the breastplate of righteousness. It protects our heart from evil and deception. You cannot walk in righteousness unless you know the Word of God. It is important to know who you are in the site of God; to think and act like He does, to believe about yourself the way He believes about you. If you don't know the Word of God how are you going to know what God thinks about you?

So get into the Word and put on your breastplate of righteousness; you will be glad you did.

The shoes of peace: the shoes of a Roman soldier were a very important part of his armament. They were made out of leather and metal, they had spikes on the bottom to keep him sure footed on all types of terrain.

The shoes of the Roman soldier began at the knees; these were called the greaves. They were made of metal and wrapped around their calves.

In addition to the spikes on the bottom of the shoes, there were two pointier spikes extended out at the front of the shoe.

When Paul wrote a bout the shoes of peace, he was talking about walking in the peace of God. When you are walking in the peace of God and it is active in your life, the enemy won't be able to hit you with the cares of life.

In Colossians 3:15 it talks about the peace of God. It says (NLT)

> *And let the peace that comes from Christ rule in your hearts. For as members of one body you are called to live in peace. And always be thankful* (My emphasis).

You have to take time to be alone with God to receive His peace. You should never go a whole day without spending time with God and His Word.

You need to learn to let the peace of God rule in your life; another words let it be the umpire in everything you do. If you don't have that peace then don't do whatever you're thinking about doing. Take time to to pray before you act.

You accomplish this peace by obeying Colossians 3:16 which says (NLT)

> *Let the message about Christ, in all its richness, fill your lives. Teach and consul each other with all the wisdom he gives. Sing psalms and hymns and spiritual songs to God with thankful hearts* (My emphasis).

Shield of faith: the Roman soldiers shield was a long and wide shield, when raised up in front of him it covered him entirely. It was made of leather; it was treated with oil and water to keep it very tight. When they went into a battle they would soak the shield with water. By doing this, when the enemy's arrows, usually flaming arrows, would hit the shield and bounce off, but sometimes they stuck, these arrows would be put out quickly due to the wet shield covering.

> Ephesians 6:16 (NLT) *In addition to all these, hold up the shield of faith to stop the fiery arrows of the devil* (My emphasis).

Keep your shield of faith up and in front of you to cover you completely, so you can quench all the fiery darts of the enemy. It's your choice to either use your shield of faith or not to use it. If you don't use it you will go through life unprotected.

Don't go into battle without your shield of faith; if you do you will regret it. It's imperative to take your shield of faith to battle.

Helmet of salvation: the Roman soldiers helmet was made of metal and was very heavy; it was also very decorative; with feathers or horsehair on top of the helmet. It was very difficult to penetrate with a sword or a battle ax.

> Ephesians 6:17 (NLT) *And take the helmet of salvation* (My emphasis).

The helmet of salvation protects your mind from the enemies relentless attacks against your mind.

Our helmet of salvation is compared to the Roman soldiers helmet because; the gift of salvation is the most beautiful gift we have.

If you leave your mind open to the attacks of the enemy he will have access to your thoughts; the control center of your mind.

Once he has access, he will keep throwing thought after thought after thought, accusation after accusation, lie after lie! Soon these thoughts will become strongholds. When they become strongholds they are much more difficult to recover from.

So don't allow cracks (little sins) in your helmet. Do not give him access!

The sword of the Spirit: the Roman sword was a dagger like sword; it was about 19 inches long, both edges were razor-sharp. It was not meant for slicing, but rather to thrust into the enemy.

Ephesians 6:17 (NLT) *And take the sword of the Spirit, which is the Word of God* (My emphasis).

God has given us a very powerful offensive weapon; His Word! Gods Word coming out your mouth frightens the devil like you wouldn't believe. It will tear them to shreds!

There are two definitions for the Word of God; first, the *logos*; the written Word of God. And then the second, *rhema;* the spoken word.

The spoken rhema when you are under attack, will put the enemy on the run. At the onset of the attack the Holy Spirit will quicken a word in your spirit and when it comes up; declare it out of your mouth!

This is what Jesus did three times when He was tempted of the devil. Each time He spoke a rhema given him by the Holy Spirit, and each time the devil could not withstand it; finally he left for another opportune time. This tells me he will flee but he will always try again.

The Lance: this is our seventh spiritual weapon; although not specifically mentioned with the other weapons, Paul said, "put on the whole armor of God." This is our final weapon.

The Roman soldier also carried with him lances. They were used to throw from my long distance to take out as many of the enemy as they could, before going into close combat.

It was a long spear like rod that could be thrown from a long distance.

Like the Roman soldiers lance; our long distance weapon is listed Ephesians 6:18.

Ephesians 6:18 (NLT). *Pray in the Spirit at all times and on every occasion. Stay alert and be persistent in your prayers for all believers everywhere* (My emphasis).

Prayer gives us an extreme spiritual power to use against the enemy. Prayer gives us the ability to stop attacks; sometimes before they even happen. If you are going to be in a situation where you know you are going to face resistance; first shower the atmosphere with prayer. Many times you will be able to ward off the attack in advance.

There are different types of prayer, some of these are; *the prayer of faith, the prayer of agreement, the prayer of intercession, the prayer of supplication, the prayer of petition, the prayer of consecration, the prayer of Thanksgiving, United prayer,* and others.

So win the battles you face with these spiritual weapons; which are both offensive and defensive. You can learn to win the battles every time.

CHAPTER 9

MORE THAN A CONQUEROR

Romans 8:35-37 (NLT) *Can anything, ever separate us from Christ's love? Does it mean he no longer loves us if we have trouble or calamity, or are persecuted, or hungry, or destitute, or in danger, or threatened with death?*

As the Scriptures say, "for your sake we are killed every day; we are being slaughtered like sheep.

"No, despite all these things, overwhelming victory is ours through Christ, who loved us (My emphasis).

What could anyone do to anyone who is not afraid of anything, not even death. There's nothing you can do to such a person; this is a great picture of Paul, who let nothing stop him!

Before I became a Christian the only time I felt like more than a conqueror was when I was in the Marines. It was during the Vietnam War; being a Marine during wartime, it is almost a sure bet that you will be going into combat.

But in my case, this isn't what the Marines wanted me to do. But after all my basic training I felt like I could conquer anything; physically and mentally.

After I came home for the Marines I got married and we had two children. The devil must've known that God had a calling on my life. And he was not happy about it.

For some reason, I was unable to hold down employment; for a short time I worked in a die casting company. One evening while I was on the machine the injection rod blew and spewed molten zinc on me; as if this wasn't enough, the machine went off again, this time the die was already full from the first injection. So when the machine went off again the metal had nowhere to go except out; spraying me with even more hot metal.

I was taken to the hospital with first, second and third degree burns over 60 percent of my body; I was also given skin grafts and was in the hospital for two weeks.

Then, two years later I came down with schizophrenia and at the end result of my psychotic episode; I shot myself under my jaw with a 12gauge shotgun.

Then years later he inflected me with two heart attacks. The devil has tried to take me out on many occasions; the Bible says; many are the afflictions of the righteous but the Lord delivers them out of them all. Psalms 34: 19.

Today, I just laugh at the devil; I tell him, "you should have taken me out when you had the chance! Now I am going to tell everyone about the one who you hate the most; Jesus my Lord."

You can read my story in my first book which is mentioned above.

When you became a Christian, God provided you with everything you need to be successful. You just need to follow the principles that He has set down; these are not suggestions, they are mandatory if you want to be more than a conqueror.

CHAPTER 10

RENDERING EVIL FOR EVIL

1 Thessalonians 5:15 (NLT). *See that no one pays back evil for evil, but always try to do good to each other and to all people* (My emphasis).

I remember a time when I had a friend that I used to drive to the bank once a month. It was a 10 to 15 minute drive to pick them up, and because of the bank they went to, it was another 15 minute drive. Then I would drive this person all over the area to pay their bills.

One day when we finished everything, I said to the person, "I want to go to such and such restaurant to have breakfast." My friend said, very sarcastically, "all you ever want to do is go to that place!"

I kept my composure, and said calmly, "I am taking you home."

My friend never said a word all the way to there house. It is sad to say, "but I have never spoken to this person again."

The next day this person kept coming to my mind, again and again. I kept pushing my thoughts down and eventually I thought of this person less and less.

About a week went by and the Holy Spirit kept saying to me; "do not render evil for evil." So, I looked up the Scripture; sure enough, it said; "see that no one pays evil for evil, but always try to do good to each other and to all people."

By this time, I had put enough distance between what happened and what I did. I knew I was wrong, but my pride got in the way. Pride always has a way of doing things like this, if you'll let it.

I finally got up to nerve to call this person, but they would not answer. The end result was, we never spoke to each other again.

Because of my pride, I lost a valuable friend, it is truly sad.

When Paul said to the Thessalonian church, "do not render evil for evil, but always do good to each other and to every person." He wasn't just asking, he was giving a strict command.

I realized, I had been inundated to the world for so long in the past to do evil for evil, that it almost became natural. I allowed my flesh to get in the way.

But I'm grateful that the Holy Spirit did not let me get away with this; he kept reminding me. As hard as I tried to push it down, it just kept coming up; I just had to deal with it once and for all.

Yes, it cost me a dear friend; but I was able to grow through it; I'm grateful for that.

Recently another thing happened where I could have rendered evil for evil. I was missing several items from my apartment. The enemy told me, it was my friend that took them. Yes, this person had the opportunity, but I had no proof whatsoever.

My friend denied they took these things and they left my apartment angry (I can't really blame them).

We didn't speak for a couple of days and it was eating at my spirit. I knew I had no proof. So, what was I going to do? A couple of days later I saw them in the parking lot, so I called them over, I asked them, "how are you doing?" They were friendly and said, "how could you think that I took them, I'm your best friend!"

I said, why don't we just let it go, and start over again from here.

Our friendship is back to normal. Only because I didn't allow the enemy to continue this masquerade of rendering evil for evil.

But, if that first incident had never happened, I might have lost this friend.

CHAPTER 11

VESSELS

THE BODY OF CHRIST

Paul uses two metaphors to tell us about the body of Christ. One is in 2 Timothy. The second is found in 1 Corinthians.

We'll talk first about 2 Timothy 2:20 (NLT)

> *In a wealthy home some utensils are made of gold and silver, and some are made of wood and clay. The expensive utensils are used for special occasions, and the cheap ones are for everyday use (My emphasis).*

I have never been a guest in a wealthy person's home. I'm sure that if I was invited for the very first time, they might treat me as a special guest. Maybe bringing out the gold leaf China and expensive silverware.

On the other hand, if I was a neighbor who visited frequently, the wealthy owner would bring out the every day silverware and dishes.

Or maybe, you've been to a museum where there are many very ancient artifacts. You would find in a museum like this; artifacts of gold and silver and wood and clay.

Or, if you were to buy such artifacts, the gold and silver would be more expensive than others. But artifacts of wood and clay from ancient times are not cheap to purchase either. In a buyers mind they are both valuable.

To God, we are more valuable to Him than any gold, silver, wood or clay. We are also very valuable to the body of Christ; no matter what our calling is.

We all have different callings, but are members of one body. This brings us to the second metaphor found in 1 Corinthians, where Paul is speaking about the body of Christ, using a metaphor of our body members.

> 1 Corinthians 12:12, 15-20 (NLT). *The human body has many parts, but the many parts make up one whole body. So it is with the body of Christ.*
>
> *Some of us are Jews, some are Gentiles, some are slaves, and some are free. But we have all been baptized into one body by one Spirit, and we all share the same Spirit*
>
> *Yes, the body has many different parts, not just one part.*
>
> *If the foot says, "I am not a part of the body because I am not the hand," that does not make it any less a part of the body.*

And if the ear says, "I am not part of the body because I am not the eye," would that make it any less a part of the body?

If the whole body were an eye, how would you hear? Or if your whole body were a ear, how would you smell anything?

But our bodies have many parts, and God has put each part just where he wants it.

How strange a body would be if it had only one part.

Yes, there are many parts, but only one body.

Remember: you are valuable right where you are!

CHAPTER 13

The battle is the Lord's

Are you fighting battles you have no business fighting? I'm going to tell you a couple of stories from the Bible.

We find this story in 2 Chronicles, we will start verse 13 (NIV)

All the men of Judah, with their wives and children and little ones, stood there before the Lord.

Then the spirit of the Lord came upon Jahaziel son of Zachariah, the son of Benaiah the son of Jeiel, the son of Mattaniah, a Levite and descendant of Asaph, as he stood in the assembly.

He said, "listen, King Jehoshaphat and all who live in Judah and Jerusalem! **This is what the Lord says to you: do not be afraid or discouraged because of this vast army. For the battle is not yours, but God's.**

Tomorrow March down against them. They will be comming up by the pass of Ziz, and you will find them at the end of the gorge in the desert of Jeruel.

You will not have to fight this battle; take up your position; stand firm and see the deliverance the Lord will give you, all Judah and Jerusalem. Do not be afraid; do not be discouraged. Go out to face them tomorrow, and the Lord will be with you."

We will go down to verse 20.

Early in the morning they left for the desert of Tekoa. As they set out, Jehoshaphat stood and said, "Judah and the people of Jerusalem! Have faith in the Lord your God and you will be upheld; have faith in his prophet's and you will be successful."

After consulting the people, Jehoshaphat appointed men to sing to the Lord and to praise him for the splendor of his holiness as they went out at the head of the Army, saying: "give thanks to the Lord, for his love endures forever."

As they began to sing and praise, the Lord sat ambushes against the men of Ammon and Moab and Mount Seir to destroy and annihilate them. After they finished slaughtering the men from Seir, they helped by destroying one another.

When the men of Judah came to the place that over-looks the desert and walked toward the vast army, they saw only dead bodies lying on the ground; no one had escaped.

If that does it increase your faith! Then, I'll tell you another story. We will start in 2 Kings 19:4 (NLT)

But perhaps the Lord your God has heard the Assyrian chief of staff, sent by the king to deify the living God, and will punish him for his words. Also pray for those of us who are left!

After King Hezekiah's officials delivered the king's message to Isaiah, the prophet replied, "say to your master, this is what the Lord says: do not be disturbed by this blasphemous speech against me from the Assyrian kings messengers.

Listen, I myself will move against him. And the King will receive a message that he is needed at home. So he will return to his land, where I will have him killed with a sword."

Meanwhile, the Assyrian Chief of Staff left Jerusalem and went to consult the king of Assyria, who had left Lachish and was attacking Libnah.

Soon afterward King Sennacherib received word that King Tirhakah of Ethiopia was leading an army to fight against him. Before leaving to meet the attack, he sent messengers back to Hezekiah and Jerusalem with this message:

This message is for King Hezekiah of Judah. Don't let your God, in whom you trust, deceive you with promises that Jerusalem will not be captured by the king of Assyria.

You know perfectly well what the kings of Assyria had done wherever they have gone. They have completely destroyed everyone who stood in their way! Why should you be any different?

Have the gods of other nations rescued them, such nations as Gozan, Haran, Rezeph, and the people of Eden who were in Tel-assar? My predecessors destroyed them all!

What happened to the King of Hamath and the king of Arpad? What happened to the kings of Sepharvaim, Hena, and Ivvah?

After Hezekiah received the letter from the messengers and read it, he went up to the Lord's temple and spread out before the Lord.

And Hezekiah prayed this prayer before the Lord. "Oh Lord, God of Israel, you are enthroned between the mighty cherubim! You alone are God of all the kingdoms of the earth. You alone created the heavens and the earth. Come down, oh Lord, and listen! Open your eyes oh Lord and see! Listen to Sennacherib's words of defiance against the living God.

Then Isaiah son of a Amoz sent this message to Hezekiah: "this is what the Lord, the God of Israel, says: I have heard your prayer about King Sennacherib of Assyria

and the Lord has spoken his word against him: the virgin daughter of Zion despises you and laughs at you.

The daughter of Jerusalem shakes her head in derision as you flee.

Who have you been obeying and ridiculed? Again, so did you raise your voice?

At whom did you look with such haughty eyes? It was a Holy one of Israel!

By your messengers you have defied the Lord. You have said, "with my many chariots I have conquered the highest mountains yes, the remote is peace of Lebanon, I have cut down the tallest cedars and it's finest cypress trees. I have reached its farthest corners and explored its steepness for us.

I had dug wells in many foreign lands and refreshed myself with their water. With the sole of my foot I stopped up all the rivers of the Egypt!

But have you heard? **I decided this long ago. Long ago I planed it**, *and now I am making it happen. I planed for you to crush fortified cities into heaps and rubble.*

That is why their people have so little power and are so frightened and confused. They are as weak as grass, as easily trampled as tender green shoots. They are like grass sprouting on the house top, scorched before it can grow lush and tall.

But I know you well, where you stay and when you come and go. I know the way you have raged against me.

And because of your raging against Me and your arrogance, which I have heard for Myself, I will put My hook in your nose and My bit in your mouth. I will make you return by the same road in which you came.

Then Isaiah said to Hezekiah, here is the proof that what I say is true: this year you will eat only what grows up by itself, and next year you will eat what springs up from that. But in the third year you will plant crops and harvest them, you will tend vineyards and eat their fruit.

And you who are left in Judah, will have escaped to the savages of the siege, will put roots down in your own soil and will grow up and flourish. For a remnant of my people will spread out from Jerusalem, a group of survivors from Mount Zion. The passionate commitment of the Lord of heavens armies will make this happen

and this is what the Lord says about the king of Assyria: his armies will not enter Jerusalem. They will not even shoot an arrow at it. They will not march outside its gates with their shields nor build banks of earth against its walls.

The king will return to his own country by the same road on which he came he will not enter the city, says the Lord. Now for My own honor and for the sake of My servant David, I will defend this city and protect it.

That night the angel of the Lord went out to the Assyrian camp and killed a 185,000 Assyrian soldiers. When the surviving Assyrians woke up the next morning, they found corpses everywhere.

Then Sennacherib of Assyria broke camp and returned to his own land. He went home to his capital of Nistoch and stayed there.

One day while he was worshiping in the Temple of his God Niscosh, his sons Adeammwlwch and Sharezer killed him with their swords. They then escaped to the land of Ararat, and another son Esarhaddon became the next king of Assyria (My emphasis).

I realize I wrote a lot of versus from these two stories. I wanted to get across to you, that God is for you, and not against you!

To protect Israel, in first story; he had the enemy, all destroy each other. In the second story; he sent, **ONE,** that's right, one Angel who killed 185,000 of the enemy.

God will do whatever it takes to protect you. There are some battles we are not to fight.

Do what God has told you to do; go to the doctor, get an attorney, whatever he's told you to do, do it! Then leave the rest to him.

1 Peter 5:7 (AMP) Says; *casting all your cares[all your anxieties, all your worries, and all your concerns, once and for all] on Him, for He cares about you[with deepest affection, and watches over you very carefully]* (My emphasis).

Don't try to carry the load all by yourself; give it to Jesus.

CHAPTER 14

DID JESUS WANT TO RESURRECT LAZARUS?

Every sermon I have ever heard talking about the resurrection of Lazarus said; that Jesus waited on purpose so He could resurrect Lazarus.

I read another teaching, that makes more sense to me. Jesus loved Lazarus! I do not believe he waited intentionally not to go and heal Lazarus. Jesus loved him and wanted to go heal him.

The reason he did not go, was that; there were Jews who wanted to kill Jesus. When they heard that Lazarus was sick, they went to Lazarus' house and lie in wait for Jesus to come heal him.

But, the Holy Spirit who knows everything; forbid Jesus to go. While He tarried, Lazarus died.

When the Jews, realized that Lazarus died, they said; "there is no reason for us to stay, Lazarus has died, and Jesus will not be coming to heal him." So they left.

They did not consider a resurrection.

The Holy Spirit, then told Jesus; "go and resurrect Lazarus from the dead."

This story, makes a lot more sense to me, then what I've always heard.

You decide for yourself, which story to believe.

CHAPTER 15

BE FAITHFUL UNTIL THE END

In Revelation 2:10 we read; (NLT)

> *Don't be afraid of what you are about to suffer. The devil will throw some of you into prison to test you. You will suffer for 10 days. But if you remain faithful, even when facing death, I will give you the crown of life* (My emphasis).

If you are in a position where you are facing something that seems unbearable; just know that all of us face these situations in life.

Look at what the people in Revelation 2 were facing. But even facing death Jesus told them to remain faithful.

Jesus said; Matthew 24:4,5 (NLT)

Jesus told them, don't let anyone mislead you for many
will come in my name, claiming, "I am the Messiah."
They will deceive many. (My emphasis).

Jesus was telling them (His disciples) the things that would occur in the end of days. There will be great deception, and even Paul and Peter prophesied that the world as a whole would be deceived on a large scale.

Jesus gave them specific signs that would mark the end of this age. He gave them a clear warning of a large-scale deception that would occur in the last days. He told them it is necessary for people to prepare and guard against this. He said in verse 4.

Take heed that no man deceive you (My emphasis).

We can see it in today's society; a great deception, where good is called evil, and evil is called good. Were the truth is called a lie, and a lie the truth. We can all see this, even here in America.

Are you aware that there are people, Christians, who are being imprisoned and persecuted and even put to death! In other countries.

There was actually more Christians put to death in the last century than in any other century. Difficult to believe, huh. But it's true.

We most likely won't see this here in America. But already, even here; the church is under attack by the enemy.

Will we be willing to go through persecution; of the likes that we have never seen?

The government wants to tax ministries and churches that are spreading the good news.

So many of them don't like our message of love, and kindness, and goodness and most of all forgiveness.

The truth is; that the church is what's holding back the evil from a full scale attack.

> James 5:16 (NIV) *The prayer of a righteous person is powerful and effective* (My emphasis).

The time is now; to pray like we never prayed before!

We don't know when the end will come, one thing is certain we are in the end of the end days. Are you willing to stay faithful even to the end? This is what Jesus is asking us.

CHAPTER 16

A FIRM FOUNDATION

How many of you have seen a building being built? Did you notice the foundation? That is the most crucial part of the building. The taller the building the deeper the foundation.

What is your foundation built on? I hope it's on Christ!

> 1 Corinthians 3:11 (NLT) *For no one can lay any foundation other than the one we already have: Jesus Christ.*
>
> *Anyone who builds on that foundation may use a variety of materials gold, silver, jewels, wood, hay, or straw.*
>
> *But on the judgment day, fire will reveal what kind of work each builder has done* (My emphasis).

Take very good care of what you build on this foundation; because they will be tried by fire! This fire will reveal what you built on this foundation.

I don't know about you, but I'm looking forward to rewards. So, I'm trying to do my best to use the best materials. I base those materials on the Word of God. I'm still growing and may never reach the full stature of Jesus; but I am being very teachable and studying and practicing.

Like I mentioned before; how bad do you want it?

I know I mentioned these things before. But they are so vitally important. I want to mention them again and this time add to it.

> 1 Corinthians 3:14(NLT) *If the work survives, that builder will receive a reward.*
>
> *But if the work is burned up, the builder will suffer great loss. The builder will be saved, but like someone barely escaping through a wall of flames* (My emphasis).

Jesus said; a man that built his house on the rock survived the storm. The one who built on sand his house fell.

We know this is a true statement because Jesus said so. But were not talking about the foundation, we are talking about what was built upon it.

Our foundation is strong and will last forever. For what we build on it, is what will be tested. Did you build on the foundation with gold, silver and jewels? Or did you build on it with wood, hay and stubble?

If you built with wood, hay and stubble; one match will set the whole thing a blaze!

Did you do what Jesus asked you to do? Did you go where he asked you to go? Did you love when he asked you to love? Did you forgive me asked you to forgive? Did you give money when he told you to give? My friend, the day is coming and is fast approaching when our works will be tried with fire.

Everything were supposed to do is all in the book; I suggest, that you read and study and follow it. It has the power to save your soul!

He has the book. Nothing is hid that won't be revealed. My suggestion is, take a good look at what you're building with.

It's not too late to start rebuilding on your foundation. Ask the Holy Spirit, he will give you what you need to know.

Jesus wants to give you rewards. But it's up to us to build His way.

CHAPTER 17

Do not consider yourself more spiritual than others!

1 Corinthians 4:7 (NLT) *For what gives you the right to make such a judgment? What do you have that God has not given you? And if everything you have is from God, why boast as though it were not a gift* (My emphasis).

This kind of thinking is nothing but spiritual pride; and I don't mean the spirit of the Holy Spirit!

I have actually known people like this; in the church, of all places. They'll be walking by and you say hello and they act like; who are you to say hi to me! This is wrong.

If you are further along in spiritual matters and gifts, it's not your job to snub people.

Rather, it's our job to teach them what we know. An act of arrogance will only push people away from Christ. We are supposed to bring people to Christ.

Jesus was meek and humble; he went about doing good, healing and delivering people.

There was never a more meek and humble person then Jesus. And we are called to imitate him. If you are going to be spiritually arrogant; He might take even that which you have.

God is not mocked; what you sow you shall also reap. This is not a maybe, it's a spiritual law.

So when you present yourself to others, then afterwords, judge yourselves, if you said and did the right things.

The Holy Spirit will tell you what you did right and what you did wrong. So, it's very important to learn the voice of the Spirit.

If you're arrogant and rude you'll get a sour taste in your mouth and a bitter stomach. He'll let you know what you did, what you said and how you said it.

If the taste in your mouth is sweet, and your stomach is not bitter; then you did and said the right thing. Do not let spiritual superiority be said of you.

CHAPTER 18

THOUGHTS AND EMOTIONS

Have you come to the realization that, your life goes in the direction of your thoughts and emotions.

If you don't get your thoughts and emotions kept in check, they will control your life.

Have you ever noticed the more you dwell on a issue in your life, such as a problem, a lack of finances or a health issue, the larger these issues become.

If you don't make up your mind to deal with these issues at the start, when they first manifest, they will more than likely come to pass in your life.

If it's a problem, it gets bigger and bigger. If it's lack of finances, you end up in a lack. If it's a health problem, that health problem can actually be harder to treat and to be healed.

What I am writing is true for anyone who does not control their thoughts and emotions.

So, if this is true in the negative then it will also be true in the positive. Get your thoughts going in a positive direction. Yes, this problem is big, but my God is bigger. Yes, my finances are low, but God will meet all my needs according to His riches in glory by Christ Jesus. Yes, they said I have a health issue, but I was healed by the stripes of Jesus, God is restoring health back to me. No weapon formed against me shall prosper! **"No weapon!"**

Get your words, thoughts and emotions in agreement with your faith.

Before I learned all this, I had great difficulty dealing with these types of issues. As I mentioned earlier, I have a psychiatric disorder. And before I came to the Lord, and getting on the correct medication, these kinds of problems controlled me to the point where I would push them aside and not even deal with them.

The only thing was, by doing this, the issues never went away, they just compounded.

This is when the mental health people, doctors and social workers had to get involved to get me out of it.

The issues that I let get out of hand put me in a dangerous position; you see, I had a alcohol and substance abuse problem. So, at times I would depend on that to self medicate, only making matters worse.

Finally, I was put on a different medication, and wa la, it was like a whole new world. My life drastically changed for the better. But, like I mentioned near the beginning of this book, I stopped my medication when I was born again.

This is when I knew I had to stay on my medication if I wanted a normal life.

Now, with the medication and being born again, reading the Bible, Christian books and listening to Christian teaching my life has turned 180 degrees for the better.

Now I tear down those thoughts and emotions that don't line up with the word of God. I use spiritual weapons, not carnal. I bring those thoughts and emotions into captivity unto the obedience of Christ.

It takes practice, but it works.

TEMPTATIONS

You have to understand that any temptation you face is common.

Paul wrote in 1 Corinthians 10:13 (NLT)

> *The temptations in your life are no different from what others experience. And God is faithful. He will not allow the temptation to be more than you can stand. When you are tempted, he will show you a way out so that you can endure* (My emphasis).

A temptation is not like anything else; it starts in the mind and emotions. If you deal with it with the first onset of the thought you can stop it in the bud, before it gets out of hand.

Now that you're a Christian, it's not like you don't have any supernatural help. You have the Holy Spirit and the name of Jesus! With them, you can stop any temptation before it becomes a problem.

When you're beginning to get tempted, listen closely to the Holy Spirit; he will show you the way out.

Know before hand that the flesh is going to want its way. You have to remain strong and courageous. If you do, the temptation will pass and won't cause any damage.

CHAPTER 19

BELIEVERS AUTHORITY

There are two kingdoms, I am not talking about the kingdoms of the earth, (nations).

(1); The kingdom of darkness (Satan's kingdom). And (2); The kingdom of light (kingdom of His dear Son).

When God created the earth and the first human being, Adam. He gave Adam dominion (authority) over the entire earth.

When Adam disobeyed God and ate of the forbidden fruit from the tree of the Knowledge of Good and Evil; he committed treason.

By committing this treason Satan usurped authority and dominion over the earth.

After Adam committed treason God spoke to Adam's wife, Eve, and told her that her seed would crush the serpent's head and the serpent would bruise her seeds heel.

Satan heard this conversation, and from that point onward he was looking to destroy this seed when he came.

Approximately 3974 years later the angel, Gabriel, was sent to Mary. He told Mary; "you will bear a son, and you will name him

Jesus. He will be great and will be called the Son of the Most High." You can read the entire exchange in (Luke 1: 26-38).

Satan now knew who the seed was and was obsessed with destroying Him. His **first** attempt was when Jesus was a child. He put fear in the heart of King Herod, who thought this child (King) would take away his kingdom. So, he ordered the death of all babies two years old and younger in and around Bethlehem. But, an Angel warned Joseph and Mary of this plot; they took Jesus to Egypt until they were told to return.

Fast-forward 30 years; Jesus is now ready to start His ministry, but first, after His baptism, He was lead into the wilderness where He was tempted of the devil.

After beating Satan on all three of his temptations; Jesus came out of the wilderness with all the power of the Holy Spirit.

> Acts 10:38 (NLT) *And you know that God anointed Jesus of Nazareth with the Holy Spirit and with power. Then Jesus went a round doing good and healing all who were oppressed of the devil, for God was with him* (My emphasis).

Satan had never dealt with anyone like this man Jesus. Jesus whipped him at every turn!

He was totally unraveling all the authority that Satan possessed over people. Remember that saying; there's a new sheriff in town.

Satan had to come up with a plan to destroy Jesus. So, he first started riling up the religious folks; the Pharisees and Sadducees. Satan had them attempt to kill Jesus several times, but it didn't work, because it wasn't Jesus's time yet to be glorified.

Then after three years it was Jesus's time to be lifted up. The end began when Satan got into Judas, one of Jesus' 12 disciples, and convinced him to betray Jesus.

Judas went to the high priest and sold out Jesus for 30 pieces of silver. The high priest and his subordinates, along with Judas. Came up with a plan to arrest and to crucify Jesus.

I'm sure you know how they did arrest Jesus, how they brought Him before the Sanhedrin, mocked Him, beat Him, and spit on Him! And how they then brought Him before Pilate, who questioned Jesus. Pilate found no guilt in Jesus and wanted to release Him, but to satisfy the Jews, he first scourged Jesus. Pilate thought this would pacify the Jews, but they insisted and threatened Pilate with being a traitor to Rome. Due to the pressure, Pilate released Jesus to be crucified.

They crucified the King of glory! Satan thought he had finally got rid of Jesus; his plan had worked. At least that's how it looked to Satan, but in reality, it was God's plan all along. Three days later He resurrected Jesus, raising Him up in victory over death, hell and the grave.

By now, you are probably wondering where I am going with this. Because, the title of this chapter is the believers authority. I first had to lay the foundation for where I'm going next.

In Matthew 28:18 (NLT) it says;

Jesus came and told his disciples, "I have been given all authority in heaven and on earth." (My emphasis).

These were some of the last words that Jesus spoke to his disciples at His ascension.

In Acts 1:4-5 it says (NLT)

Once when he was eating with them, he commanded them, "do not leave Jerusalem until the Father sends you the gift He promised, as I told you before.

John baptized with water but in just a few days you will be baptized with the Holy Spirit.", (My emphasis).

Jesus was talking of the coming day of Pentecost, when that day finally came they were all filled with the Holy Spirit.

From that day till the present born-again believers, when they receive Christ, are indwell-ed with the Holy Spirit.

What happens to us positionally when this occurs?

When Christ ascended, He gave all His authority to the Church, which of course, is the body of Christ in the earth.

When Christ ascended, the Father seated Him at His own right hand, where we know there is no higher authority. (What I say next is very important!) **We have been seated with Him, on His throne.**

When Christ was raised, we were raised with Him. This is not something that's going to happen in the bye and bye. **It has already occurred.**

Paul said in Ephesians 1:18-23 (NLT)

I pray that your hearts will be flooded with light so that you can understand the confident hope He has given to those He called His holy people who are His rich and glorious inheritance.

I also pray that you will understand the incredible greatness of God's power for us who believe Him. This is the same mighty power that raised Christ from the dead and seated Him in the place of honor at God's right hand in the heavenly realms.

Now He is far above any ruler or authority or power or leader or anything else not only in this world but also in the world to come.

God has put all things under the authority of Christ and has made Him head over all things for the benefit of the Church.

And the Church is His body; it is made full and complete by Christ, who fills all things everywhere with Himself (My emphasis).

Satan tried to stop the resurrection. But his forces were confounded and confused and were defeated by our Lord Jesus Christ!

Colossians 2:15 (NLT) *In this way, He disarmed the spiritual rulers and authorities. He shamed them publicly by His victory over them on the cross* (My emphasis).

Ephesians 6:12 (NLT) *For we are not fighting against flesh and blood enemies, but against evil rulers and authorities of the unseen world, and against evil spirits in the heavenly places* (My emphasis).

Anytime you get into a battle with the enemy, remember; you have authority over them. It's also important to be covered with all your armor; which I wrote about earlier.

Revelation 5:10 (NKJV) *And have made us kings and priests to our God; and we shall reign on earth* (My emphasis).

If we don't have authority, how can we possibly reign on earth as kings and priests?

CHAPTER 20

LAST OF THE LAST DAYS

What does God's Word say about the last days? 2 Timothy 3:1-9 (NLT)

You should know this, Timothy, that in the last days there will be very difficult, (perilous), times.

For people will love only themselves and their money. They will be boastful and proud, scoffing at God, disobedient to their parents, and ungrateful. They will consider nothing sacred.

They will be unloving and unforgiving; they will slander others and have no self-control. They will be cruel and hate what is good.

They will betray their friends, be reckless, puffed up with pride, and love pleasure rather than God.

They will act religious, but they will reject the power that could make them godly. Stay away from people like that!

They are the kind who work their way into people's homes and when the confidence of vulnerable women who are burdened with the guilt of sin and controlled by various desires.

(Such women are forever following new teachings, but they are never able to understand the truth).

These teachers opposed the truth just as Jannes and Jambres opposed Moses. They have depraved minds and counterfeit faith.

But they won't get away with this for long. Some day everyone will recognize what fools they are, just as with Jannes and Jambres (My emphasis).

My brothers and sisters, we see these kinds of people, at least I do, in my every day walk of life. We are beginning to live in the times Paul prophesied about so long ago.

As rendered in the original Greek; the Holy Spirit is telling us that we must know what He is telling us, it's critical that we know this.

The world around us is falling into depravity, (moral corruption and wickedness), at an alarming rate!

There are so many people afraid of doing many things due to a fear of what might happen. I'm talking about things people never had a fear of doing or going.

All they hear about is school shootings, church shootings, food market shootings, department store shootings, people in cars running over pedestrians, drive-by shootings and these aren't the half of it. It's getting crazy!

These things are some of the reasons why we as believers have to be strong and courageous and take authority over the powers of darkness in our sphere of influence.

Days are going to grow even darker, we as children of light must help bring a generation of the lost to the knowledge of the love of Christ. There is only one hope for the world of the lost; that's Jesus Christ our Lord!

In these verses in 2 Timothy we must understand the Holy Spirit is telling us, the generation that sees these things happening ever increasingly, they will know that they have crossed the line into the end of the end times. I believe the they in that sentence is us.

CHAPTER 21

A SOVEREIGN GOD

When I was considering to write this chapter on a Sovereign God, I had a lot of questions. I meditated on this for days, because I just did not know how to explain it.

David said in Psalms 139:16 (NLT)

You saw me before I was born. Every day of my life was recorded in your book. Every moment was laid out before a single day had past.

Isaiah 46:10 (NLT) *Only I can tell you the future before it even happens. Everything I plan will come to pass, for I do whatever I wish.*

Colossians 1:16-17 (NLT) *For through him God created everything in the heavenly realms and on earth. He made the things we can see and the things we can't see such as thrones, kingdoms, rulers and authorities in the unseen world. Everything was created through him and for him.*

Isaiah 45:7 (NKJV) *I form the light and create darkness, I make peace and create calamity; "I the Lord do all these things"* (My emphasis).

Do you see why I wrote, I don't know how to explain it. The truth is; God cannot be fully explained. But one fact remains: "God is **LOVE!**"

If you were to try to comprehend everything that God is you would go insane.

Romans 11:33-36 (NLT). *Oh, how great are God's riches and wisdom and knowledge! How **impossible** it is for us to understand his decisions and his ways!*

For who can know the Lord's thoughts? Who knows enough to give him advice?

And who has given him so much that he needs to pay it back?

For everything comes from him and exists by his power and intended for his glory. All glory to him forever! Amen (My emphasis).

Yes, God created everything, both good and bad. He created it, but that doesn't mean He initiates it (talking about evil). If it's good, then He initiated it.

If it's bad or evil then it's from the devil. I wrote earlier, that the devil only comes to steal kill and destroy! That's **ALL** he comes for.

My very first pastor said something very profound; *"the devil can be one of God's greatest refining tools."* You're asking; "God can use the devil?" I believe he can, if it's going to work out for a person's good. Remember? I wrote; All things work for good; for those that love God and are called according to His purpose (Romans 8:28). Don't worry; God will only let the devil go so far and no further.

GIVING THE SECRET TO INCREASE

Most people, especially those who are new to the things of God, would question; "how could I possibly increase by giving away?" The truth is, in the beginning we all have questioned the things of God and His ways of doing things.

The Bible is very clear, in Isaiah 55:8,9 (NLT) the word of the Lord says:

> *"my thoughts are nothing like your thoughts," says the Lord. "And my ways are far beyond anything you can imagine." For just as the heavens are higher than the earth, so my ways are higher than your ways and my thoughts higher than your thoughts.* (My emphasis).

So, how do we begin to know the thoughts and ways of God? The answer is: by reading and studying His word, reading books and listening to sound teachings. Most of all, become sensitive to the Holy Spirit and His leading.

These are accomplished by what is taught in Romans 12:2 *(NLT)*

> *don't copy the behavior and customs of this world, but let God transform you into a new person by changing the way you think. Then you will learn to know God's*

will for you, which is good and pleasing and perfect. (My emphasis).

Of course, learning the above covers all areas of life, but I am going to be talking about financial increase and how giving can bring increase.

God has set up laws, both in the physical realm and the spiritual realm. A couple of the physical laws are, the law of gravity, the laws of aerodynamics, the laws of physics and the laws of mathematics.

One spiritual law is the law of faith. But, there is one I want to focus in on that is both physical and spiritual:

It is the law of sowing and reaping. When a farmer sows seeds he expects, at harvest time, to reap abundantly more than he sowed. The same is true spiritually; when we sow financially, over time, (known as seed, time and harvest), we will receive much more than we sowed. If we do this consistently we will begin a continuous cycle of increase in our lives.

One particular verse in the word of God speaks about this cycle of increase. It's found in Amos 9:13 (MSG)

> *"things are going to happen so fast your head will swim, one thing fast on the heels of the other. You won't be able to keep up. Everything will be happening at once and everywhere you look, blessings! Blessings like wine pouring off the mountains and hills. I'll make everything right again for my people"*

This process happens supernaturally. Something happens in the spiritual realm; its a spiritual law. I don't understand it, but it works. It's worked time and again in my own life. It will work, not only for the believer, but will also work for someone not saved; because it is a spiritual law.

To begin, there are two things we must get established and settled in our hearts and our minds. 1st: everything belongs to God; He owns it all. In Ps 50:12b (KJV) it says:

for the world is mine, and the fullness thereof.

Again, in Hag 2:8 (KJV) it says:

the silver is mine, and the gold is mine, saith the Lord of hosts. (My emphasis).

2nd. King David understood this; after he and his people had given billions of dollars in gold and silver and everything needed to build the temple; he said in 1 Ch 29:14

but who am I, and who are my people, that we give anything to You? Everything we have has come from You, and we give You what You first gave us! (My emphasis).

Now that we have come to the understanding that it all belongs to God. We can start to look at ourselves as stewards; caretakers of what God has given to us.

In Mat 10:8 (KJV), Jesus is talking to his disciples about going out and healing the sick, cleansing the lepers, raising the dead and casting out devils. He said:

freely ye have received, freely give. (My emphasis).

I believe this can also be said about freely giving of our finances.

Joal 9:23- 27 (NLT). *Rejoice, you people of Jerusalem! Rejoice in the Lord your God! For the rain he sends demonstrates his faithfulness. Once more the autumn rains will come as well as the rains of spring.*

The threshing floors will again be piled high with grain, and the presses will overflow with knew wine and the olive oil.

The Lord says, "I will give you back which you lost in the swarming locusts, the hopping locusts, the stripping locusts and the cutting locusts It was I who sent this great destroying army against you.

Once again you will have all the food you want, and you will praise the Lord your God, who does these miracles for you. Never again will my people be disgraced.

Then you will know that I am among my people Israel, that I am the Lord your God, and there is no other. Never again will my people be disgraced

This accelerated harvest includes more than souls. His promises also include our finances.

Don't allow lack by holding back.

Psalm 126:5,6 (NLT). *Those who planted in tears will harvest with shouts of joy.*

They weep as they go to plant their seed, but they sing as they return with the harvest.

Proverbs 28:20 (NLT). *The trustworthy person will get a rich reward, but a person who wants quick riches will get into trouble.*

Psalms 92:12, 14 (NLT). *But the Godly will flourish like palm trees and grow strong like the Cedars of Lebanon.*

Even in old age they will still produce fruit; they will remain vital and green.

TITHING

The tithe is 10 percent of your income. The only place in Scripture where God says to prove Him is in Malachi 3 and it is concerning the tithe.

He says in Malachi 3:10-12 (NLT)

> *bring all the tithes into the storehouse so there will be enough food in My Temple. If you do, says the Lord of heaven's armies", " I will open the windows of heaven for you, I will pour out a blessing so great you won't have room enough to take it in! Try; put me to the test!"*
>
> *"Your crops will be abundant, for I will guard them from insects and disease. Your grapes will not fall from the vine before they are ripe," says the Lord of heaven's armies.*
>
> *"Then all nations will call you blessed, for your land will be such a delight," says the Lord of the heavens armies* (My emphasis).

In all probability, there will be times when the enemy has a impasse into an area of our lives. Although it will appear as a setback, in reality it is a set up for God to bring us up higher.

In Psalms 34:19 (NLT) it says:

the righteous person faces many troubles, but the Lord comes to the rescue each time.

And again, in Psalms 91:3 (NLT) it says:

for he will rescue you from every trap and protect you from deadly disease.

In Romans we have this promise, it says in Romans 8:28 (KJV):

and we know that all things work together for good to them that love God, to them who are called according to His purpose. (My emphasis).

Malachi 3:9, God told His people they were cursed with a curse, because they robbed Him of His tithe and offerings.

Now we know that we are no longer under the curse of the law because of the sacrifice of our Lord Jesus. But the promises of God remain in tact.

2 Corinthians 1:20 (KJV) says: *for all the promises of God in Him are yea, and in Him Amen, unto the glory of God by us.* (My emphasis).

So the promise of God opening up the windows of heaven and pouring us out a blessing that we won't have room enough to receive is for us today; the condition is we pay our tithes and offerings.

Now, I have learned not to put God in a box. He is God and He does what He wants to do, but I have also learned that He cannot go against His word. If His word says to do this and if you do, then this will happen; then that's exactly what will happen. It just may not happen the way you thought.

I am sure there are many people for whom God has opened the windows of heaven and yet they never paid their tithe.

> Romans 9:15 (KJV) says: *for he saith to Moses, I will have mercy on whom I will have mercy, and I will have compassion on whom I will have compassion.* (My emphasis).

There are those who believe that tithing is Old Testament only and not part of the New Covenant. I wonder if they use this as an excuse not to tithe? Why would you not want to tithe? considering the blessing that comes with it.

There is only one place in the New Testament that I know of where tithing is mentioned. It is in Matthew 23:23 (NLT) which says: Jesus speaking,

> *"what sorrow awaits you teachers of righteousness and you Pharisees. For you are careful to tithe even the tiniest income from your gardens, but you ignore the more important aspects of the law; justice, mercy, and faith. You should tithe, yes, but do not neglect the more important things."* (My emphasis).

So Jesus is telling the scribes and Pharisees they did right to tithe but should not have forgotten the other commandments of the law. We cannot expect to receive a blessing for paying our tithe and go out and live our lives in an unchristian manner, lacking mercy and compassion for others. We are to love our neighbors as ourselves.

When you have began tithing you may not necessarily see increase right away. There may be times of testing, God is seeing if you're really committed and also because He has to start working things out in the spirit realm. Moving people and situations on your behalf.

Also, expect the enemy to come against you, telling you that tithing doesn't work; that you are wasting your time. But the enemy is a liar and him coming against you should be a sign that your doing the right thing.

It says in Galatians 6:9: (NLT)

> *so let's not get tired of doing what is good. At just the right time we will reap a harvest of blessing if you don't give up.* (My emphasis).

Dig your heels in and stay committed.

While you are waiting keep an open mind, the increase may not come as cash dollars, it may, but it may not. It may come as an idea or opportunity such as; a job opportunity, business venture, book idea, a stock to invest in, a job promotion. God has innumerable ways to bring you your blessings, so be sensitive to His Holy Spirit.

Understand that the blessings may come progressively, over a period of weeks months or years. This is how it's been for me. A little more increase with each new level. Seven years ago I was homeless, I did not have a penny to my name and I mean that literally. God was faithful and kept me off the street.

When I began to get some income I began to tithe. It was a struggle for a while, but the following year my Social Security disability was reinstated.

I was able to get my own apartment, and three years after that I received my veterans service-connected disability.

I am not a rich person by any means, but I am considered middle-class and making more money now than in my entire life and I don't have to go out and work.

I have another claim in with the VA for retroactive disability, when that goes through I will receive a check that is in the six figures.

> Psalms 84:11 (KJV) says, *for the Lord God is a sun and shield: the Lord will give grace and glory: no good thing will he withhold from them that walk uprightly.* (My emphasis).

Israel were not His children; they were His servants. Now that we are on the other side of the cross; we are no longer servants, we are children. How much more pleasure does God have? Now that we have become His children!

I am a firm believer that the tithe should go to your home church, but if you do not yet have one, then give to a ministry that feeds your spirit until you have a home church.

Before I go on to Giving, you might be asking, how do I know tithing and giving works? First: because it says so in God's word, Numbers 23:19 (KJV) says:

> *God is not a man, that He should lie; neither the son of man, that He should repent: has He said, and shall He not do it? Or has He spoken, and shall He not make it good?* (My emphasis).

Secondly: it is a supernatural spiritual principle or law; just like the law of gravity or the laws of physics; it works every time! And lastly: I testify that it has worked in my own life.

GIVING

When I refer to giving, I am also referring to offerings. And I'm referring to it being above what you give as tithe. Unless you are in such a tight financial condition that you can't pay your tithe, then give some type of offering.

> Pr 3:9-10 (KJV) says: *Honor the Lord with thy substance, and with the first fruits of all thine increase: so shall thy barns be filled with plenty, and thy presses shall burst out with new wine.* (My emphasis).

If we would honor the Lord with our substance and get into the habit of giving of all our increase (yes, above our tithe). We would experience a life without lack.

What is the purpose of God blessing us? We are a conduit in which blessings flow. The blessings flow to us and then flow from us; to be a blessing to others.

I am not saying we have to give our entire blessing away. Rather, it works as reciprocity, the practice of exchanging things with others for mutual benefit.

In Luke 6:38(KJV) Jesus said:

> *"give, and it shall be given unto you; good measure, pressed down, shaken together, and running over, shall men give into your bosom."* (My emphasis).

Consider your finances as seed to be planted to bring a harvest, the greater the seed the greater the harvest. The harvest always brings more than the seed sown.

Paul said in 2 Corinthians 9:6: (NLT)

> *remember this; a farmer who plants only a few seeds will get a small crop. But the one who plants generously will get a generous crop.* (My emphasis).

As you begin to give of your finances, and the Lord begins to bless you, consider giving more. When you decide to give more, scatter your seed. Give to different ministries.

> Proverbs 11:24, (NLT) says: *give freely and become more wealthy; be stingy and lose everything.* (My emphasis). This is saying,the more seed you scatter the more you will increase. The more you withhold the less you will have.

Oral Roberts said: "if you have a need, sow a seed". You can not buy a miracle and you cannot bribe God, but you can show God your faith through your works.

In this case giving is your works. James 2:17-36 (NLT) says:

> *so you see, faith by itself isn't enough. Unless it produces good deeds, it is dead and useless.*
>
> *Now someone may argue, "some people have faith; others have good deeds." But I say, "how can you show me your faith if you don't have good deeds? I will show you my faith by my good deeds."*
>
> *You say you have faith, for you believe that there is one God. Good for you! Even the demons believe this, and they tremble in terror.*

How foolish! Can't you see that faith without good deeds is useless?

Don't you remember that our ancestor Abraham was shown to be right with God by his actions when he offered his son Isaac on the altar?

You see, his faith and his actions worked together. His actions made his faith complete.

And so it happened just as the Scriptures say; "Abraham believed God, and God counted it as righteous because of his faith." He was even called the friend of God.

So you see, we are shown to be right with God by what we do, not by faith alone.

Rahab the prostitute is another example. She was shown to be right with God by her actions when she hid those messengers and sent them safely away by a different road.

Just as the body is dead without breath, so also faith is dead without good works. (My emphasis).

Hebrews 11:6-13 (NLT) says: *and it is impossible to please God without faith. Anyone who wants to come to Him must believe that God exists and that He rewards those who sincerely seek Him.*

It was by faith that Noah built a large boat to save his family from the flood. He obeyed God, who warned him about things that have never happened before. By his faith Noah condemned the rest of the world, and he received the righteousness that comes by faith.

It was faith that Abraham obeyed when God called him to leave home and go to another land that God would give him as his inheritance. He went without knowing where he was going.

And when he reached the land God promised him, he lived there by faith for he was like a foreigner, living in tents.

And so did Isaac and Jacob, who inherited the same promise.

Abraham was confidently looking forward to a city with eternal foundations, a city designed and built by God.

It was by faith that even Sarah was able to have a child, though she was barren and was too old. She believed that God would keep his promise.

And so a whole nation came from this one man who was as good as dead a nation with so many people that, like the stars in the sky and the sand on the seashore, there is no way to count them.

All these people died still believing what God had promised them. They did not receive what was promised, but they saw it all from a distance and welcomed it. They agreed that they were foreigners and nomads here on earth.

Obviously people who say such things are looking forward to a country they can call their own. And if they had longed for the country they came from, they could've gone back.

But they were looking for a better place, a heavenly homeland. That is why God is not ashamed to be called their God, for He has prepared a city for them.

It was by a faith that Abraham offered Isaac as a sacrifice when God was testing him. Abraham, who had received God's promises, was ready to sacrifice his only son, Isaac.

Even though God had told him, "Isaac is his son through whom your descendants will be counted."

Abraham reasoned that if Isaac died, God was able to bring him back to life again. And in a sense, Abraham did receive his son back from the dead.

It was by faith that Isaac promised blessings for the future to his sons, Jacob and Esau.

It was by faith that Jacob, when he was old and dying, blessed each of Joseph's sons and bowed in worship as he leaned on his staff.

It was by faith that Joseph, when he was about to die, said confidently that the people of Israel would leave Egypt. He commanded them to take his bones with them when they left.

It was by faith that Moses parents hid him for three months when he was born. They saw that God had given them an unusual child, and they were not afraid to disobey the king's command.

It's was by faith that Moses, when he grew up, refused to be called the son of Pharaoh's daughter.

He chose to share the oppression of God's people instead of enjoying the fleeting pleasures of sin.

He thought it was better to suffer for the sake of Christ than to own all the treasures of Egypt, for he was looking ahead to his great reward.

It was by faith that Moses left the land of Egypt, not fearing the king's anger. He kept right on going because he kept his eyes on the one who is invisible.

It was by faith that Moses commanded the people of Israel to keep the Passover and to sprinkle blonde on the doorposts so that the angel of death would not kill their firstborn sons.

It was by faith that the people of Israel went right through the Red Sea as though they were on dry ground. But when the Egyptians tried to follow, they were all drowned.

It was by faith that the people of Israel marched around Jericho for seven days, and the walls came crashing down.

It was by faith that Rahab the prostitute who was not destroyed with the people in her city who refused to obey God. For she had given a friendly welcome to the spies.

How much more do I need to say? It would take too long to recount the stories of the faith of Gideon, Barak, Samson, Jephthah, David, Samuel, and all the prophets.

By faith these people overthrew kingdoms, ruled with justice, and received what God had promised. Worked righteousness, obtained promises, stopped the mouth of Lions, quenched the flames of fire, escaped death by the edge of the sword, out of weakness were made strong, became valiant in battle, turn to flight the armies of the aliens.

Women received their loved ones back again from death. But others were tortured, refusing to turn from God in order to be set free. They placed their hope in a better life after the resurrection.

Some were jeered at, and their backs were cut open with whips. Others were chained in prisons.

Some died by stoning, some were sawed in half, and others were killed with the sword. Some went about wearing skins of sheep and goats, destitute and oppressed and mistreated.

All these people earned a good reputation because of their faith, yet none of them received all that God had promised

for God had something better in mind for us, so that they would not reach perfection without us (My emphasis). See how important faith with works is?

Proverbs 3:9 –10 says: *honor the Lord with thy substance, and with the first fruits of all thine increase: so shall thy barns be filled with plenty, and thy presses shall burst out with new* wine. (My emphasis).

If you are giving of your finances you will never lack. In John 15:7 Jesus said:

if ye abide in me, and my words abide in you, ye shall ask what ye want and it will be done unto you (Emphasis added).

If you ask and it doesn't come to pass it may be that you are asking amiss. James 4:3, says:

ye ask, and receive not, because ye ask amiss, that ye may consume it upon your lusts (My emphasis).

God wants you to have nice things, He just doesn't want things to have you.

2 Corinthians 9:10 says: *now He that ministerth seed to the sower both minister bread for your food, and multiply your seed sown, and increase the fruits of your* righteousness (My emphasis).

When God sees that you are serious about doing business with him He will provide the seed.

In Proverbs 13:22b it says: *and the wealth of the sinner is laid up for the just* (Emphasis added). He will take from the sinner and give it to you, the just.

Ecclesiastics 11:1 says: *cast thy bread on the waters: for thou shall find it after many* days. (My emphasis).

If you don't see results right away continue doing what you're doing and increase will come. The hard part is the waiting.

Psalm 112 (NASB). *Praise the Lord! How blessed is the man who fears the Lord. Who greatly delights in His commandments.*

His descendants will be mighty on earth; the generation of the upright will be blessed.

Wealth and riches are in his house. And his righteousness endures forever.

Light arises in the darkness for the upright; he is gracious and compassionate and righteous.

It is well with the man who is gracious and lends; he will maintain his cause in judgment.

For he will never be shaken; the righteous will be remembered for ever.

He will not fear evil tidings; his heart is steadfast, trusting in the Lord.

His heart is upheld, he will not fear. Until he looks with satisfaction on his adversaries.

He has given freely to the poor; his righteousness endures forever; his horn will be exalted in honor.

The wicked will see it and be vexed; he will gnash his teeth and melt away; the desire of the wicked will perish.

Psalms 37:4 says: *delight thyself also in the Lord; and he shall give thee the desires of your heart.* (My emphasis).

Just put God first.

Jesus said in Luke 12:34:

for where your treasure is, there will your heart be also (My emphasis. Make God your treasure.)

If you follow these principles you will begin a cycle in your life of sowing and reaping, and at some point the reaping will overtake the sowing:

as it says in Amos 9:13:

behold, the days come, saith the Lord, that the plowman shall overtake the reaper, and the treader of grapes him that soweth seed (Emphasis added). I wrote this Scripture earlier; this is the King James version.

And also in Deuteronomy 28:1,2 it says:

and it shall come to pass, if thou shalt hearken diligently unto the voice of the Lord thy God, to observe and to do all his commandments which I command thee this day, that the Lord thy God will set thee on high above all nations of the earth: and all these blessings shall come on thee, and overtake thee, if thou shalt hearken unto the voice of the Lord thy God (Emphasis added).

Now we know the Lord is speaking of the commandments of the law, but I am convinced that if we follow these principles of tithing and giving, then the blessings of increase will come upon us and overtake us, too.

PARTNERSHIPS

Partnerships are vital; they are the life blood to any ministry.

Even Jesus had partners; He not only had the twelve disciples and the seventy He commissioned. But there were many others who ministered unto His needs as He traveled from city to city. Providing a place to stay, food, drink and finances.

We know for a fact that Jesus received finances because he had a treasurer; Judas Iscariot, he held the money bag; as recorded in John 12:4-6.

I believe that many others that He healed and cast out the demons from; such as Mary Magdalene had also become His partners.

In the book of Philippians Paul was writing to the Philippian church.

He writes in Philippians 4:19 (KJV)

but my God shall supply all your need according to his riches in glory by Christ Jesus (My emphasis).

He wrote this because no other church communicated (partnered) with him concerning giving and receiving, but them only; verse 4:15.

Then in verse 4:17 he says: *not because I desire a gift: but I desire fruit that may abound to your account* (My emphasis).

What account is he speaking about? Our heavenly account.

Because we give to the poor and have partnerships with ministries that give to the poor and preach the gospel; we are laying up for ourselves a treasure in heaven.

Having God supply all our needs is a wonderful promise, but I believe I am like most others when I say; "I want much more than my needs met."

You may not be aware of it, but God wants that for you too. Psalms 35:27 (KJV) says:

let those who favor my righteous cause and have pleasure in my uprightness shout for joy and be glad and say continually, let the Lord be magnified, who takes pleasure in the prosperity of his servant (now we are children) (My emphasis).

Also, in Ephesians 3:20 (KJV) it says:

but to him that is able to do far exceedingly above all which we ask or think, according to the power which works in us (My emphasis).

What is that power that works in us; The Holy Spirit. I'll close with this Scripture, 2 Corinthians 9:7 (KJV):

every man according as he purposeth in his heart, so let him give; not grudgingly, or of necessity: for God loveth a cheerful giver (My emphasis).

CONCLUSION

I have come to the close of this book. I have written on many different Christian topics and Christian principles. I have tried my best to back everything up with Scriptures. For I feel very strongly that, **Scripture has the final say.**

As you live and grow in your Christian faith you will have many ups and downs. Many may be very difficult, you will go through many that are fiery trials; but Jesus warned us about this; he said, "in this life you will have trouble, but be of good cheer; I have overcome the world." For me, when I went through these trials, I promise you, I did not have good cheer. It wasn't until I went through them and looked back, only then could I see that Jesus was there the whole time. And then when I went to the next one, it was a little easier; and each time they got easier and easier. I'm not saying they were fun because they weren't. But my trust in God grew and grew and grew.

I will give you one of my testimonies of how; you may give up on a dream that God has put in your heart, but God doesn't forget and He doesn't give up; I know this for a fact.

Shortly after I was released from the psychiatric hospital in 1984 God put on my heart to file for service-connected VA disability.

So I did, expecting it all to go well, because God had put on my heart. But, I was denied. I appealed, again I was denied. Then in 1989 I appealed again, again I was denied.

I wanted to appeal again, but my service officer said, "I was beating a dead horse and that I would never get it!" So I laid it to rest, buried it, accepting it was over.

Then, 30 years later, from my first attempt in 1984 I met a woman attorney; she said, "let's try again." I said, "I have tried time and time again, it just won't go through."

So I came home and that evening I was sitting in my chair; I heard an audible voice in my right ear. He said, "service-connected." I knew that it was God, so the next day I went back to the attorney and agreed to file again.

The attorney was able to get me an evaluation from a psychiatrist well-versed in VA law. I met with him about six times and he also met with my brother; about my behavior when I came home from the Marine Corps. I also gave the psychiatrist two affidavits; one from my mother-in-law, and one for my lifelong family friend.

After reviewing all the evidence and my entire VA file; the doctor came to the conclusion that my disability began shortly before I came home for discharge from the Marine Corps.

With this report and the stages of schizophrenia onset; we filed my claim with the VA. The VA law judge sent me to a VA psychiatrist who agreed with my psychiatrist and he said, "it was as likely as not that my disability began in the Marine Corps. VA law states; if the evidence presented weighs 50-50; then the presumption of the evidence goes to the veteran.

Jesus had won! I will tell you; any battle the Lord fights, He does not lose.

God kept his promise even though it took 30 years: He doesn't forget!

I have to correct an error. I said, "your thoughts and emotions begin in your brain: I was wrong. They begin in your heart. This is verified not only by Scripture but also verified by medical science. The Scripture is found in Proverbs 4:23 (KJV).

> *Keep thy heart with all diligence; for out of it are the issues of life* (My emphasis).

If you don't believe what I have written in this book; then believe the Scriptures! If you still don't believe; then this book isn't for you. It's for believers!

ABOUT THE AUTHOR

Edward LaPointe is a 74-year-old born-again Christian since 1998. Edward served in the United States Marine Corps from 1969 to 1971; a Vietnam era veteran.

He has no seminary credentials, he just loves the Lord and the Lord's Word. Since his conversion he can testify of the Lord's faithfulness even in the worst of times. The Lord has come through for him time and time again. All the glory be to his Lord and Savior Jesus.

Edward is in remission of a schizoaffective disorder. He has service-connected compensation for this disorder.

You can read his memoir in his book; ***His Grace In The Midst Of Tragedy.***

Visit Edwards website at Author Edward LaPointe. Com

www.ingramcontent.com/pod-product-compliance
Lightning Source LLC
Chambersburg PA
CBHW060932050726
47592CB00003B/920